RESUMES: THE WRITE STUFF

A QUICK GUIDE TO PRESENTING YOUR QUALIFICATIONS EFECTIVELY

by Robbie Miller Kaplan

ISBN 0-912048-47-6
Library of Congress Catalog Card Number 87-045263

Published and distributed by the Garrett Park Press
PO Box 190B
Garrett Park, MD 20896

Dedicated to Jim and to my mother—for their belief, support and love.

And to Samantha and Julie for all their cooperation which made the writing possible.

Acknowledgements

To Nancy Wallace for her assistance, encouragement, and friendship.

To Sam Sylvestore for his review and feedback.

TABLE OF CONTENTS

PREFACE

There are hundreds of resumes competing for attention. Will yours stand out from the pack?

Resume writing is a chore for many people. It doesn't have to be. After all, you are writing about your favorite subject—yourself. The process of writing a resume can be a challenging and rewarding experience. Just like any other task, it requires skills. These skills can be learned.

Hundreds of job seekers have been trained using the steps outlined in this book. Their success in the job market and their requests for a written summary of the principles I have used in their training has inspired the writing of this book.

The following chapters provide a step-by-step approach to recording your past experiences, discovering your accomplishments, and assessing their importance to your overall career plan. Valuable information, tools, and resources are presented to guide you through the writing process. You will learn by example to write and re-write a resume that will get results.

The guidelines are here. You supply the effort.

Good luck and good reading.

Robbie Miller Kaplan
Vienna, Virginia
April 1987

INTRODUCTION

"You'll have a tough time finding a position as good as the one you left." Those discouraging words came from an executive recruiter I had located through the yellow pages. He proceeded to cut my credentials to shreds and I was devastated. Salvaging what I could from the encounter, I rewrote my resume based upon his comments.

I went to the public library, researched interesting companies, and put together what I thought was a dynamite letter and resume. As I was about to begin my job campaign, I found a great job advertised in the classified section. It was as if someone had taken all of the responsibilities from my previous job and had written the ad just for me. I applied for the position and told my friends, "If I don't get an interview for this job, I will never get another interview in my life."

Unfortunately, the rejection letter arrived five days later stating that the incumbent decided not to leave the job and they would keep my resume on file. I had already addressed a letter to the same company and I decided to go ahead and mail it anyway. After all, they might have other jobs.

A few days later, I received a mailgram requesting that I call personnel immediately to arrange an interview. I found those instructions easy to take and after four hours of interviews realized that this was the same job that had been advertised.

I was offered, accepted the position, and got the job because my letter and resume stood out. They had filtered to the hiring manager along with a penciled notation, "Call her, she looks good."

In another position, I spent 40% of my time recruiting and sometimes interviewed ten people in one day. I helped many candidates with their approach in hopes that they would be better prepared for the next interview. I often wanted to say, "You didn't get the job, but this is what you should do so you can get the next job."

When it was time for me to make a career change, I decided to use my expertise to inspire others to view job hunting as a positive and enriching experience.

Looking for a job can be exciting. Planning a job search and having a sense of control wards off some of the feelings of rejection that are inevitable in a job hunt. Knowing that you are presenting your qualifications in the most favorable light will give you confidence throughout your job campaign.

CHAPTER 1

TO DO OR NOT TO DO? THAT IS THE QUESTION

What Is a Resume?

A resume is not an autobiography, nor is it a chronicle of all of your experiences. It should summarize experiences relevant to your career goals, highlight your accomplishments, and show what you learned from those experiences.

The resume is a marketing tool. It should sell you to prospective employers the same way an advertisement entices you to purchase a product. It is the first impression employers will have of you and from it, they will decide if they ever want to meet you.

There is no right or wrong way to write a resume—only a better way. Your resume is as individual as you are and needs to be designed to express your unique qualities. Copying a canned resume format or content will not work as it probably won't highlight your skills and abilities to your advantage.

The format of your resume should be carefully considered and developed. Ask yourself, "How will this information look best?", "What qualifications are most important for this career area?"

Resumes don't get jobs but resumes can open or close the door to job opportunities. The goal of the resume is to make the employer want to talk with you—to make you one of the select group to whom job interviews are offered.

A resume should not be a once in a lifetime experience. You may need to develop several resumes as part of a current job search—if you are applying for more than one type of position. As you gain new experiences, develop different career goals, or advance to higher levels of work, you will draft different resumes. But, the basic principles remain the same and the techniques highlighted in this book should help throughout your working career.

Types of Resumes

The two basic types of resumes are the chronological and the functional.

The **chronological resume** is a summary of your education and experience in date order beginning with the most recent and working backwards. This form works best for an individual who has followed a specific career plan with jobs of increased responsibility.

Some employers will only accept chronological resumes.

This type of resume does not work well for an individual with frequent job changes, gaps in employment history, or someone who wishes to use skills acquired in nonwork settings, such as volunteer activities, to emphasize qualifications for employment.

The **functional resume** highlights your skills and experience in specific areas such as administration, communications, marketing, management, or planning. It may or may not include a work history.

In the past, personnel managers felt individuals were hiding something when they used a functional resume. In recent years it has become an accepted form and can be very effective for:

—individuals who are re-entering after a work gap
—those who have or will be changing careers
—individuals who have been in the same or similar positions for a long period and the work responsbilities are repetitive when listed chronologically.

The Essentials

Most resumes include some or all of the following:

1. **Name, complete mailing address, and phone number, including area code.** If possible, also include your business number. The more accessible you are, the more likely you will be reached.

2. A **Career objective** that indicates the kind of job you are seeking. It should be specific enough to imply that you know what you are looking for, but not so specific that you won't be considered for a broader range of positions. Avoid pronouns. They make an objective sound self serving. Employers want to know what you can do for them, not what they can do for you.

3. **Education**
   —If high school is your last graduation, include that.
   —If you graduated from a college or technical school, go back no further.
   —If you have an Associate's degree and a Bachelor's degree, include both.
   —If you have Associate's, Bachelor's and Master's degrees, include the Bachelor's and Master's only.
   —If you have a Doctor's degree, include your Bachelor's, Master's, and Doctor's degrees, but go back no further.
   —Give title of major field or fields, subject of any major research, date of graduation or completion, academic honors (if any), or major activities while in school.

4. **Employer related training and additional courses.** Attendance at formal courses or on-the-job training received in current or past employment.

5. **Work experience or history**, including skills and accomplishments. As important as what you did is how well you performed, so emphasize your unique accomplishments.

6. **Professional associations and memberships.**

7. **Professional licenses, honors, publications, and certifications.**

8. Specific **skills** that you have such as typing, shorthand, and language fluency. Stress those related to your career goal. It may not help to stress scuba diving skills if you are interested in a technical research position.

The Optionals

The following are areas you might want to consider. Beware of wasting space. Choose only those areas that will enhance your qualifications.

1. **Personal Data**
   It is illegal for an employer to ask about your age, marital status, and children. Why offer any information that would give someone the opportunity to discriminate against you? It is in your best interest to offer information on your resume that shows you to be the most qualified candidate. For all information you plan to include, ask yourself, "Does this information make me a better candidate?" If not, don't include it. Use every bit of available space to market yourself.

   Have you ever heard of anyone writing: Health: Poor?

2. **Hobbies and Interests**
   Unless you have had unusual accomplishments in hobbies or interests, don't include them. Save this information for the application or the interview. **DO** use this area if a hobby or interest shows great accomplishment or can be tied into the position you are seeking.

3. **References**
   At the time of a job interview, you will be asked for the names of your references, so why waste a line of space that reads

   References Furnished Upon Request

   when you can use the space to market yourself. I always suggest eliminating this line on your resume. Many experts disagree. But, we all agree that it doesn't make sense to waste valuable space by listing names, titles, addresses, and phone numbers of people prepared to comment on your qualifications. Besides using valuable space, you run the risk that many prospective employers will call your references. If you abuse your references, you may lose them. Use your references only for positions you are really interested in obtaining. Be sure to contact your references ahead of time to discuss positions of interest. It is helpful to send them a copy of your resume to reinforce your skills and accomplishments. This may assist them in responding to inquiries.

4. Summary

A summary can be used as a capsule of experience. It gets the message across. Use for extensive work experience or to highlight a particular skill or area of interest. Some individuals prefer to use a summary instead of a career objective. The summary can be called; Career History, Career Highlights, Summary of Experience, or Career Summary.

A summary works well for people such as:

—Persons with 20 or more years of military experience. A few opening sentences show a wide variety of experience and accomplishments.

—Individuals who have changed careers. A resume might not flow smoothly and a summary states up front what you want an employer to know.

—Those with experience in both the public and private sector. The summary will pull it all together.

Isn't There a Law Against That?

The Civil Rights Act of 1964 prohibits discrimination on the basis of color, race, sex, religion, or national origin in employment decisions by employers, employment agencies and labor organizations who have 15 or more employees. A 1972 amendment brought the federal government under the act and prohibits discrimination of individuals because of pregnancy, childbirth, or related medical conditions.

The Age Discrimination in Employment Act, passed in 1967 and amended in 1979, protects individuals over age 40 to age 70, against discrimination based on age. Employers who have 12 or more employees are affected.

Handicapped persons are protected under the Rehabilitation Act of 1973, if they are able to perform the job. Only firms that get federal money are affected.

Question: I am a member of a minority group. Should I send a picture with my resume so that I might get employment priority?

Answer: No. While the law offers you equality, the truth is that many people are prejudiced. Why give someone information that is not required and give them the opportunity to discriminate against you without even meeting you.

Question: I know it is illegal for an employer to ask about marriage and children but some employers discriminate against women with children. Should I indicate on my resume that I am married and childless?

Answer: No. If an employer doesn't want to hire women with children, he or she may still discriminate against you. Just because you don't have children now doesn't mean you don't plan on having them in the future.

Great Beginnings

There is an old Chinese proverb that "A long journey begins with but a single step." Often the hardest part of developing the resume is to take that first step. It is easier if you can organize your efforts by following the steps listed below.

Step 1

Sit down and chronologically list all of your work experience—paid and unpaid. Consider fraternal, military, community, religious, and educational.

Even if you have extensive paid experience, list your unpaid experience as well. Most people use skills and abilities they really enjoy in their volunteer activities. In outlining these experiences, you may see a trend that you can translate into related experiences helpful in your job hunt.

For example:

Work Experience

1984 – present	American Medical Association	Personnel Recruiter
1982 – 1984	American Medical Association	Personnel Assistant
1983 – 1984	Valley Community Library	Volunteer Coordinator
1981 – present	United Church	Newsletter Editor
1979 – 1982	Valley Community Hospital	Personnel Assistant
1976 – 1979	Valley Community Hospital	Personnel Secretary
1974 – 1977	Valley Community Hospital	Gift Shop Aide
1970 – 1976	Jones, Williams, Inc.	Secretary
1968 – 1970	Davis Community College	Yearbook Staff

Useful Sources of Information

It is hard to remember all the job information you will need to outline your experience. Go through your records and look for:

1. Job advertisements . . . yours or similar ones.
2. Job descriptions.
3. Standards of performance.
4. Performance evaluations.
5. Offer letters.
6. Letters of commendation.
7. Certificates of completion.

Step 2

Once you have listed all of your work experience in order, take a separate sheet of paper for each experience and develop a complete list of responsibilities.

For example:

Personnel Recruiter Responsibilities

1. Recruit staff.
2. Affirmative Action Coordinator.
3. College Campus Representative.
4. Administer appropriate tests.
5. Develop and update orientation program.

6. Give orientation presentations.
7. Thorough familiarity with organizational structure and personnel policies to present to prospective employees.
8. Liaison with the community.

Step 3

Take separate sheets of paper for each area of responsibility. List all the tasks required to carry out that responsibility.

For example:

Responsibility: Recruit Staff

Tasks

1. Research local publications for most appropriate to place classified ads.
2. Write ads for classifieds.
3. Place ads in publications.
4. Work with local college placement offices to list job openings.
5. Phone screen potential candidates.
6. Set up interviews.
7. Interview candidates.
8. Check references.
9. Evaluate skills and merits of each top five candidates.
10. Rank the top five candidates.
11. Make job offers.

Step 4

It is important to show both responsibility and accomplishment. To do this, review your tasks and look at the problems, challenges, and obstacles that you have to overcome. What actions did you take to successfully complete your tasks? What did you accomplish?

For example:

Responsibility: Recruit Staff

Problem

1. Fill entry level management positions with individuals who will remain in position and be interested in career advancement.
2. Hire candidates who will be a good match to reduce turnover.

Actions Taken

1. Researched periodicals to attract most appropriate candidates.
2. Worked with local colleges.
3. Offered and gave several free speeches on job hunting techniques to get our organization's name out to the public.

Accomplishments

1. Reduced turnover by 20% through attracting, interviewing, and carefully screening a large base of qualified candidates.

Step 5

Your Education

Outline your education chronologically. Include colleges, technical or professional schools, and business or professional training. Include those completed and those in progress. List everything. You will later eliminate those that will not support your career objective.

For example:

Education

1986	Management Skills, American Medical Association
1985	Effective Business Communication, American Medical Association
1984	Management Studies, American Medical Association
1983	Effective Time Management, Adult Education
1981	Bachelor of Science in Business Administration, Ohio State University
1979	Personnel Procedures, Valley Community Hospital
1974	Secretarial Procedures, Valley Community Hospital
1970	Associate in Applied Arts, Davis Community College
1970	Effective Listening Techniques, Adult Education
1970	Speed Writing, Adult Education

The Elements, Dear Watson

The astute Sherlock Holmes and the bumbling Dr. Watson combined their talents to solve hundreds of fictional mysteries. They used a variety of research tools to outwit criminals. You need to assemble effective tools to outwit those job seekers competing with you for openings.

Tools

The essential tools are a dictionary and thesaurus. A synonym dictionary is very helpful. These will assist you in spelling and eliminating redundancy.

A handbook for grammar and punctuation is an asset. Resources are listed below. Check your library or local bookstore for additional sources.

Resources

Devlin, Joseph. **A Dictionary of Synonyms and Antonyms.** New York, New York: Warner Books, 1983.

Roget, Peter Mark. **Roget's Thesaurus of English Words and Phrases.** New York, New York: Chatham River Press, 1979.

Schell, John and Stratton, John. **Writing on the Job.** New York, New York: New American Library, 1984.

Strunk, William Jr., and White, E. B. **The Elements of Style.** New York, New York: MacMillan Publishing Co., Inc., 1979.

The Merriam-Webster Dictionary. New York, New York: Pocket Books, 1974.

Punctuation. Different elements of punctuation simplify reading and understanding. It is critically important that the reader finds your resume easy to follow. Your goal is to develop a resume that will visibly highlight your most marketable skills. Proper punctuation plays an important part in the presentation of your resume.

Semi-colon (;) is used to separate parts of equal significance.

   1. Use in a series when the items in the series already contain commas.

      For example:

      Managed office staff of five. Hired, supervised, dismissed; ordered supplies, controlled inventory, issued purchase orders; acted as manager during owner's absence.

   2. Use between two or more independent clauses when they are not connected by a coordinate conjunction (coordinate conjunctions are: and, or, but, and nor).

      For example:

      Developed a new program for typing skills; enrollment increased by 20%.

      Employment dates are listed first; names of organizations and job titles are listed second.

Hyphen (-) is found within words. There are so many rules for hyphenation that you should consult a dictionary or grammary book for correct spelling.

   For example:

   part-time   two-thirds
   long-range   all-out effort
   up-to-date   on-the-job training
   past-due account   re-create

Colon (:) is used to alert the reader that an explanation, list, enumeration, or quotation will follow.

   For example:

   Management responsibilities include: recruiting, supervising, reviewing performance, counseling, and dismissing.

Use the colon after the salutation in a business letter.

   For example:

   Dear Mr. Madison:

Comma (,) alerts the reader to a brief pause.

Use a comma:

   1. In a series of three or more words, phrases, or dependent clauses. Use between each of the items and before the coordinate conjunction that separates the last two. The comma before the coordinate conjunction is required in business writing.

      For example:

      Design, layout, and proof graphic arts for newsletter.

2. Between the individual elements in addresses and names of places.

For example:

12 Hollywood Avenue, Tuckahoe, New York 10707
Spanish internship in Madrid, Spain

Active Voice Verbs

When choosing verbs, use verbs that are in the active voice. The term **voice** refers to whether the subject of the sentence performs the action or receives it. When a subject performs the action it is in the active voice and appears in the first part of the sentence. When the subject receives the action it is in the passive voice and appears in the last part of the sentence.

For example:

Passive   Responsible for management of personnel office.
Active   Managed personnel office.

Passive   Transportation routings were developed for various classes of mail.
Active   Developed transportation routings for various classes of mail.

Passive   Handled the classification of new personnel.
Active   Classified new personnel.

Passive   Provide management, guidance, and direction to staff of five.
Active   Manage, guide, and direct staff of five.

Passive   In charge of scheduling 100 police officers.
Active   Schedule 100 police officers.

Active Verbs

administer	counsel	integrate	procure
advise	create	interview	produce
analyze	delegate	introduce	propose
anticipate	demonstrate	invent	provide
appraise	design	inventory	recommend
arrange	determine	investigate	reconcile
assess	develop	launch	record
assign	devise	lead	recruit
assist	direct	locate	represent
audit	distribute	maintain	research
brief	document	manage	resolve
budget	draft	mediate	review
calculate	edit	monitor	schedule
check	establish	negotiate	solve
classify	evaluate	operate	substantiate
coach	execute	order	supervise
collect	formulate	organize	teach
communicate	identify	originate	test
compile	implement	participate	track
compose	inform	perform	train
conceive	initiate	plan	update
conduct	inspect	prepare	utilize
consult	install	present	validiate
control	institute	prioritize	verify
coordinate	instruct	process	write

Characteristics of Active Voice

1. Forceful and direct
2. Requires fewer words
3. Shows authority
4. Easier to understand

What Do I Do Now?

You now have a written history of your experience and education. It is time to decide whether a chronological or a functional resume will highlight and market your skills and accomplishments.

Holly Wallach has six years of experience with two brokerage firms. She has been promoted three times. She plans on pursuing a management position with another brokerage firm. The chronological resume would work well for her.

Donna Webster has been a homemaker for 12 years. She has coordinated fundraising and publicity for the Red Cross and Parent Teacher Association (PTA). Donna would like to begin full-time work as a fundraising manager or public relations coordinator. A functional resume, emphasizing her skills, projects, and performance, would work best.

Henry Allen is retired. He would like to do some part-time work. He is financially secure and would like a position that ties in with his love of stamp collecting. A functional resume would draw attention to his different collections, exhibits he has created, conferences attended, articles written and published in newsletters, and association memberships.

Once you have decided the type of resume you will use, review your working papers and choose the information that best describes what you have done and what you have to offer. Most people discover they have more marketable skills than they realized. All of these will probably not go into your resume. Select information that best supports your career objective. Concentrate on clarity. Beware of writing a job description. It's not what the employer can do for you, but what you can do for the employer.

Piecing The Puzzle

The format of your resume is the way you organize information. The structure you choose should visualize your unique achievements and traits, whether they be education, skills, or experience. A resume format is as individual as you are and should reflect your personal strengths. Are you a winner? Toot your own horn. If you don't, no one else will. Play up your achievements. Stress your strong points and downplay or omit your weaknesses. Will your resume stand out against the competition?

Most hiring personnel will scan a resume rather than read it. They will scan from top to bottom. Ask yourself, "Which of my areas most qualify me for the positions I seek?" List these categories first.

All resumes should begin with name, address, phone number, and career objective (or summary). The rest of the resume can be structured at the individual's discretion. Most individuals center their name, address, and phone number. I would encourage you to be creative. There are numerous examples in the second chapter of this book of different formats and layouts. Most resumes tend to look the same—make yours eye catching. As long as it is professional, it will stand out from the pack.

Caution—don't be too creative or unusual so that your resume stands out too much. You want it to be regarded with interest, not amusement.

Check List

- Do you have highly marketable skills such as word processing, accounting, or computer programming? You might emphasize these at the top of the resume under "Skills".

- Do you have unusual or prized work history or experience? You might want to include a short "Work History" at the beginning. This can be used when a Career Objective is also present.

- Are you a recent graduate? Do your studies qualify you for a new career field, one that you don't have many years of previous work experience? You may want to begin your resume with "Education".

- Do you have a great deal of experience in your field or skills and accomplishments that qualify you for the position you seek? You may want to begin your resume with "Experience".

The Final Product

The choice of how you will present the finished resume is yours. The total amount of money spent on a completed resume does not always equal quality.

The following information will help you decide.

Type or Typeset?

Your resume will probably be re-organized and re-typed at least five times before you are satisfied with the final product. The approximate cost to typeset is $30.00 per page. The approximate cost to have it typed through a Word Processing business is $15.00 per page. For economic reasons, I would have it initially typed on a correcting typewriter or a word processor. There are many word processing services available that can be located in the classified pages of your local paper or in the yellow pages. Be a smart shopper. Understand the services you are contracting for. When it comes to the final product, the choice is personal. Ask to see samples of the print of the elements so that you can evaluate the print and how it looks. Some word processors look great—others mediocre. This is also true for electric typewriters.

Copy or Print?

Most resumes are copied rather than printed. If a good quality copier is used, the finished product can be excellent.

Resumes can be copied on individual copiers or copied and printed at local print shops. When copying yourself, ensure that the machine has proper toner and developer and that you have cleaned the platen glass so that the copies will be clear.

Resumes can also be run off individually from a word processor so that each resume will look like an original.

Check with your local print shop and word processing services to compare costs.

Paper

Resumes and cover letters are most effective when done on the same quality paper.

There are a number of options for paper selection.

Your local stationery supply store will stock 8½ by 11 inch bond paper in buff, cream, white, and pale grey colors with matching envelopes. These are good color choices. Your resume can be copied or printed on this paper and additional paper purchased for cover letters. The approximate cost for 80 sheets and 50 envelopes is $7.00.

Your local print shop will often stock the quality paper needed to copy or print your resume. Additional paper can be purchased for cover letters.

Another alternative is ordering personal business stationary, 8½ by 11 inch, matching second sheets and envelopes. Format your resume so that it can be copied or printed right on the letterhead. Use the second sheet for a second page, if needed. This choice can look extremely professional and effective. The approximate cost for 250 printed letterhead and printed envelopes is $94.00.

Twelve Tips

1. Your resume should fit on one or two pages. If you have extensive work experience, it is fine to use two. If you are a new graduate, one is considered best. I have reviewed resumes that were seven pages in length when I was desperate to fill a position. But, the competition is too fierce to chance a lengthy resume. **Never** use a two sided copier.
2. For a two page resume, always staple the pages. You do not need to number or type your name on the second page as the staple will hold them together. Do not put your resume in a folder or plastic insert as it may need to be copied and distributed.
3. The tenses should all agree. The objective should be in the present tense, present experiences in the present tense, and past experiences in the past tense. Do not shift tense.

4. If you have accomplishments in your present position that are in the past, you may want to include this information a few spaces below your current experience. This will emphasize the accomplishment and not cause a shift in tense. If you have past and present information for a functional resume, begin skill areas with the present information and follow with the past.

5. A dictionary should never leave your side. Sam Jeffries recruits for a Fortune 500 company and tosses out every resume with a misspelled word or typo. He views this as carelessness and is not interested in that trait in his employees. Always proofread for errors and check your spelling. Some culprits are hyphenated words whose meanings are changed without the hyphen. An error that once embarrassed me during a presentation was resign when it should have been re-sign.

6. Edit your resume many times to improve word choice and redundancy. Give a copy of your resume to a trusted friend to proof and highlight the redundancies. Use a synonym dictionary, dictionary, and thesaurus.

7. Avoid using jargon, acronyms, and abbreviations. You want your reader to understand what you have to say. Degrees should be written out, with the exception of the following well recognized abbreviations: MD, JD, PhD, and DDS. Be consistent. Either spell out or abbreviate all degrees.

8. Don't use flashy colors, unusual, or odd sized paper. This often will attract the wrong attention. You don't want your resume to be passed around for the wrong reasons. A large defense contractor has what they call the "Resume of the Week." They make copies of the worst resume and circulate it throughout the office. A recent one ended with the statement, "Ask me how I lost 50 pounds."

9. Pay attention to the appearance of your resume. Avoid overcrowding. Leave at least one inch margins on the top, bottom, and sides, Underline, capitalize, and use bold print for emphasis. Believe it or not, a telecommunications organization recently received a resume that was written in pencil.

10. Reading your resume must be easy on the eyes. Recruiters may read hundreds of resumes a week and this can cause eye strain. If your resume is difficult to read, for example, not enough white space or thick paragraphs, a recruiter may pass over your resume and never see your qualifications.

11. Bullets are eye catching Use a small "o" and fill in carefully with a black felt pen. Other alternatives are the asterisk (*) and the dash (—).

12. You have just gone through a great deal of effort to write your resume. File your working papers and information in an accessible location and plan on updating it each year.

It goes without saying that you should never claim degrees, work experiences, and activities that you don't or didn't have. Unfortunately, this is a growing habit and a number of resume verification firms have sprung up who are retained by employers to verify claims of college degrees, work accomplishments, or other facts.

Resumes that contain untruths are not only tossed in the wastebasket, the names of their writers may go on "bad" lists.

Questions Please

Question: What if a company I have worked for in the past has been merged or been bought out and has changed names?

Answer: Use the new name of the company and beneath it add the old name. For example:

Enterprises Unlimited
(formerly Gomez Business Consultants)

Question: Do I need a cover letter?

Answer: Never send a resume without a cover letter. The cover letter needs to effectively draw attention to your resume—one of hundreds that will be scanned.

Question: I graduated from college a long time ago. Can I eliminate the date that I received my degree? I am afraid that I will be discriminated against because of my age.

Answer: You can omit the date of your graduation, but, if you do, you run a greater risk that someone will assume that you are hiding something. They may think that you are even older than you are!

Question: I am presently pursuing a degree. Should I include this information or will recruiters be put off wondering why it isn't finished?

Answer: If the degree will be in a relevant field, I would include it. Format it the same as you would a completed degree but state — Bachelor of Arts degree in progress. Or give the date when the degree is anticipated.

Question: Should I include citizenship on my resume?

Answer: Citizenship information is usually required on a job application. It is not required on a resume but, there are instances where you might want to include it:

1. To clarify citizenship if you have studied or lived outside the United States for much of your life.
2. The company in which you are interested is a major defense contractor.

Question: I completed a one year program at a non-college professional school. I am no longer in that career field and it has no bearing on my present career objective. Do I need to include this?

Answer: No. If you feel that this program doesn't support your career goals, you don't have to include it. Be prepared to explain the one year gap and why you have omitted this from your resume. I omitted a professional school from my resume and in ten years, no one has ever questioned the one year gap.

Question: Do I list salary on my resume or send a salary history?

Answer: No. Salary is something to discuss during the interview. Some companies run classified ads requesting salary history when they have no intention of hiring. They're interested in current salaries to re-vamp their compensation plans. Even if you know this is a legitimate job opportunity, I still advise individuals not to discuss salary until you meet face-to-face.

Question: I have been out of work for nine months. How do I show or explain this work gap?

Answer: Some employers give severance and vacation pay upon termination. This time period can be added to your dates of employment and it will narrow the gap. What have you been doing during this transition period? Any professional development? Dan Adams began work on a book while he was looking for work and Jack Klein began a master's degree in his field. Both of these experiences were included on their resumes. It filled the work gap and provided interesting information to discuss during an interview. Use the following experiences to fill a work gap: consultant, self-employed, writer, student, researcher, or traveling.

Question: I have heard of a Vita or Curriculum Vitae. Do I use this or a resume?

Answer: A Vita or Curriculum Vitae is defined as an autobiographical sketch that is used for professionals such as doctors, dentists, or college professors. It includes education, publications, licensure, and board certification. For more information consult **Developing a Professional Vita or Resume** by Carl McDaniels, Garrett Park Press, Garrett Park, Maryland 20896.

Question: How far back do I go?

Answer: There is no definite answer. Ask yourself, "How relevant is the experience to the position I am seeking?" Include it if it is still valid and meaningful. Don't include it if it isn't. Experience can still be valid, but if you have more current experience, you may want to delete the older, repetitious experience.

CHAPTER 2

BEFORE AND AFTER— RESUME MAKEOVERS

A picture is worth a thousand words. I can give you all the principles in the world on writing effective resumes but if you never see them properly applied, it is difficult to envision the end result.

Marketing experts have long known the value of "before and after" pictures in revealing possibilities. Most of us can benefit from assistance and that is particularly true of resumes. Let's look at some sample resumes and see how they could be improved as a means of helping to demonstrate principles important in your own resume development.

Many of these resumes are based on actual samples brought to training classes. The real names and basic facts about the individual have been changed to protect their privacy.

For each example, an original resume is introduced. Next, comments on the resume are given to highlight weaknesses and to point out areas where they might be improved. Finally, a revised resume is presented, implementing the suggestions.

MARG GRADY SMITH

100 Maple Street
Fairfax, Virginia 22013
Home: (703) 255-0001
Work: (703) 234-0908

CAREER OBJECTIVE

Position utilizing experience as an international economist and country
risk analyst in export-oriented company.

PROFESSIONAL EXPERIENCE

FINANCIAL ECONOMIST   1979 to present
United States Bank
Washington, D. C.
> --analyzes and monitors economic and political developments in
>   23 West African countries.
> --develops balance of payments and external debt forecasts for
>   major West African markets.
> --provides policy recommendations to senior management on country
>   creditworthiness with respect to new United States Bank exposure.
> --briefs United States Bank senior management, U. S. Government
>   and foreign government officials, exporters, and bankers on
>   United States Bank country policies.
> --coordinates United States Bank lending policies in West Africa
>   with other U. S. Government agencies.
> --initiates and pursues collection efforts in cases of overdue
>   payments resulting from country economic problems.
> --assesses general techniques and standards of United States Bank
>   country risk analysis as part of economists' task force.

INTERNATIONAL ECONOMIST   1978-79
United States Government
Washington, D. C.
> --coordinated interagency actions to reduce foreign debt
>   arrears.
> --prepared briefing material for Congressional hearings on
>   on foreign debt owed to the U. S. Governement.
> --researched issues in developing countries' finance in
>   particular external indebtedness, debt reschedulings, and the
>   stablization of export earnings.
> --provided briefing materials for senior Treasury officials
>   and U. S. delegations on developing finance issues.
> --submitted quarterly reports to Congress on debt arrears and
>   answered Congressional correspondence and letters from the
>   public on this subject.

24

EDUCATION

UNIVERSITY OF VIRGINIA, Charlottesville, Virginia
        Advanced graduate studies in international economics and
        foreign affairs, Governor's Fellowship, 1976-78.
FLETCHER SCHOOL OF LAW AND DIPLOMACY, Tufts University, Medford,
    Massachusetts.
        Master of Arts in international relations, 1975.
DUKE UNIVERSITY, Durham, North Carolina.
        Bachelor of Arts in French, magna cum laude, 1974.
        Study abroad: University of Nice, France and Oxford University,
        England.

HONORS

Listing in Who's Who of American Women
United States Bank Outstanding Performance Award--1981, 1984, 1986
United States Bank Special Achievment Award--1982, 1985

PERSONAL

Born: June 11, 1946
Marital Status: Divorced
Children: 3
Health: Excellent

1. The heading takes up too much space — almost 25% of the page.

2. This sounds self serving — what can you offer the organization? Not what they can offer you!

3. Dates are hanging.

4. Responsibilities of current position should be in present tense — do not add an "s" to verbs.

5. Awkward sentence. Poor word choice.

6. This clarification adds extra words and some awkwardness — omit.

7. Typo — "on" appears twice.

8. Dashes are not visually appealing.

9. Too much white space.

10. Headings are the same type — one doesn't stand out from the other.

MARG GRADY SMITH

(1)

100 Maple Street
Fairfax, Virginia 22013
Home: (703) 255-0001
Work: (703) 234-0908

CAREER OBJECTIVE

(2) Position utilizing experience as an international economist and country risk analyst in export-oriented company.

PROFESSIONAL EXPERIENCE
(10)

FINANCIAL ECONOMIST   1979 to present (3)
United States Bank
Washington, D. C.
           --analyzes and monitors economic and political developments in
             23 West African countries.
           --develops balance of payments and external debt forecasts for
             major West African markets.
      (4) --provides policy recommendations to senior management on country
             creditworthiness with respect to new United States Bank exposure.
           --briefs United States Bank senior management, U. S. Government
             and foreign government officials, exporters, and bankers on
      (9)   United States Bank country policies.
           --coordinates United States Bank lending policies in West Africa
             with other U. S. Government agencies.
           --initiates and pursues collection efforts in cases of overdue
             payments resulting from country economic problems.
           --assesses general techniques and standards of United States Bank
             country risk analysis as part of economists' task force.

INTERNATIONAL ECONOMIST   1978-79
United States Government
Washington, D. C.
      (5) --coordinated interagency actions to reduce foreign debt
             arrears.
      (7) --prepared briefing material for Congressional hearings on
             on foreign debt owed to the U. S. Governement.
           --researched issues in developing countries' finance in
             particular external indebtedness, debt reschedulings, and the
             stablization of export earnings.
      (8) --provided briefing materials for senior Treasury officials
             and U. S. delegations on developing finance issues.
           --submitted quarterly reports to Congress on debt arrears and
             answered Congressional correspondence and letters from the
             public on this subject. (6)

26

11. The schools are too bold and overshadow the degrees.

12. Too much white space.

13. The personal data does not add to the qualifications of the individual or make her a more desirable candidate.

EDUCATION

UNIVERSITY OF VIRGINIA, Charlottesville, Virginia
(11)   Advanced graduate studies in international economics and
        foreign affairs, Governor's Fellowship, 1976-78.
FLETCHER SCHOOL OF LAW AND DIPLOMACY, Tufts University, Medford,
        Massachusetts.
        Master of Arts in international relations, 1975.
DUKE UNIVERSITY, Durham, North Carolina.
        Bachelor of Arts in French, magna cum laude, 1974.
        Study abroad: University of Nice, France and Oxford University,
        England.

HONORS

Listing in Who's Who of American Women
United States Bank Outstanding Performance Award--1981, 1984, 1986
United States Bank Special Achievment Award--1982, 1985

PERSONAL

(13)   Born: June 11, 1946
       Marital Status: Divorced
       Children: 3
       Health: Excellent

Comments: Two pages aren't necessary. The resume should be re-worded and formatted to fit on one page. Too much overall white space. Try bullets (•) instead of dashes (—).

MARG G. SMITH
100 Maple Avenue
Fairfax, Virginia 22013

Home: (703) 255-0001
Work: (703) 234-0908

Career Objective: A position requiring expertise as an international economist
and country risk analyst in an export oriented organization.

PROFESSIONAL EXPERIENCE

Financial Economist, United States Bank, Washington, D. C.
1979 - present

- Analyze and monitor economic and political developments in 23 West African countries.
- Develop balance of payments and external debt forecasts for major West African markets.
- Conduct country risk analysis and provide recommendations to senior management for new loans.
- Brief bank senior management, United States Government and foreign government officials, exporters, and bankers on bank policies.
- Coordinate lending policies in West Africa with other United States government agencies.
- Initiate and pursue collection activities for overdue payments resulting from a country's economic difficulties.
- Assess general techniques and standards of bank country risk analysis as member of Economic Task Force.

International Economist, United States Government, Washington, D. C.
1978 - 1979

- Coordinated interagency actions to reduce overdue payments on foreign debt.
- Researched developing countries' finances including external indebtedness, stabilization of export earnings and debt reschedulings.
- Prepared and provided briefing material for Congressional hearings on foreign debt owed to United States government and to senior government officials and United States delegations on developing finance issues.
- Submitted quarterly reports to Congress on delinquent loans and answered Congressional correspondence and letters from the public.

EDUCATION

University of Virginia, Charlottesville, Virginia.
Advanced graduate studies in international economics and foreign affairs.
Governor's Fellowship, 1976 - 1978.

Fletcher School of Law and Diplomacy, Tufts University, Medford, Massachusetts.
Master of Arts in international relations. 1975.

Duke University, Durham, North Carolina.
Bachelor of Arts in French, magna cum laude. 1974.

HONORS

United States Bank Outstanding Performance Award, 1981, 1984, 1986
United States Bank Special Achievement Award, 1982, 1985
Listing in Who's Who of American Women

28

RESUME

OF

LAURA CURTIN

Address: 290 Park Avenue
                        Williamstown, Virginia 22456
Telephone: (703) 450-0090
Date of Birth: January 6, 1952
Marital Status: Single

PROFESSIONAL EXPERIENCE

Marketing: Proficient in strategic planning on both the corporate
                and private industry segment; long term as well as short
                term goal targeting. Skilled in research, analysis, pro-
                duct and industry segment projections, report computation,
                and corporate orientation. Demonstrable talents in eval-
                uation and forecasting of technological innovation, en-
                vironmental and socio-economic transgressions. Developed
                analytical framework for analysis of various industries,
                determining growth potential through acquisitions, mergers,
                and technical expansion. Conducted market research in all
                phases of analysis in numerous areas, including problem and
                objective identification, market survey design, results
                evaluation, development of planning documents, goal formation,
                promotional campaign design, and implementation.

Administration: Developed optimal scheduling to increase staff effectiveness.
                Re-designed training program of staff resulting in increased
                longevity. Analyzed maintenance necessities and developed
                a schedule to routinely prevent problems.

Management: Contacted local administration to broaden employee base.
                Effective and conscientious management resulting in 19%
                increase in sales. Trained future managers. Maintained
                and managed entire product line, as well as developed and
                displayed "theme" products. Rapid comprehension and know-
                ledge of product, coupled with selling ability propelled
                standings to highest in Eastern region. Maintained strict
                accountability of inventory to a 1 % or less variance
                against a separate accounting system.

PROFESSIONAL POSITIONS

Partner, Curtin, Smith and Brams   1986
Manager, The Horseshoe Restaurant   1983-1985
Manager, Roy Ralwings Restaurant   1982
Manager, F and R Restaurant   1980-1982
Cosmetic Representative, Revlon Cosmetics   1976-1979

EDUCATION   Mater of Business Administration in Marketing, George
                Mason University, Fairfax, Virginia . December 1986.

                Bachelor of Arts in English, South Hampton College, Long
                Island, New York. June 1975.

PROFESSIONAL   American Marketing Association
AFFILIATIONS   George Mason Alumni Association

1. Don't waste space writing "resume" — It's obvious it is a resume.

2. Eliminate personal information. Ask yourself, "Does this make me more qualified for this position?"

3. Incorrect punctuation. These are separate sentences.

4. Incorrect punctuation.

5. Use semi-colon here.

6. Prepared or planned are better word choices.

7. Awkward sentences. What does it mean? What are you trying to say?

8. Work History sounds better.

9. Eliminate the month.

10. Does this add to your qualifications? Omit Alumni Association unless you are an officer.

11. Placing school and degree on same line doesn't highlight either. Use separate lines and underline or boldface one of them. Spelling error.

12. Too much white space.

13. Shift in tense.

14. Tenure is a better word choice.

15. Paragraphs are too long and difficult to read.

---

① RESUME

OF

LAURA CURTIN

Address: 290 Park Avenue
Williamstown, Virginia 22456
Telephone: (703) 450-0090
Date of Birth: January 6, 1952 ②
Marital Status: Single

PROFESSIONAL EXPERIENCE ③

Marketing: Proficient in strategic planning on both the corporate and private industry segment; long term as well as short term goal targeting. Skilled in research, analysis, product and industry segment projections, report computation, and corporate orientation. Demonstrable talents in evaluation and forecasting of technological innovation, environmental and socio-economic transgressions. Developed analytical framework for analysis of various industries, determining growth potential through acquisitions, mergers, and technical expansion. Conducted market research in all phases of analysis in numerous areas, including problem and objective identification, market survey design, results evaluation, development of planning documents, goal formation, promotional campaign design, and implementation. ④ ⑤ ⑮

Administration: Developed optimal scheduling to increase staff effectiveness. Re-designed training program of staff resulting in increased longevity. Analyzed maintenance necessities and developed a schedule to routinely prevent problems. ⑭ ⑥

Management: Contacted local administration to broaden employee base. Effective and conscientious management resulting in 19% increase in sales. Trained future managers. Maintained and managed entire product line, as well as developed and displayed "theme" products. Rapid comprehension and knowledge of product, coupled with selling ability propelled standings to highest in Eastern region. Maintained strict accountability of inventory to a 1% or less variance against a separate accounting system. ⑬ ⑫ ⑦

⑧ PROFESSIONAL POSITIONS

Partner, Curtin, Smith and Brams   1986
Manager, The Horseshoe Restaurant   1983-1985
Manager, Roy Ralwings Restaurant   1982
Manager, F and R Restaurant   1980-1982
Cosmetic Representative, Revlon Cosmetics 1976-1979

EDUCATION ⑪ Mater of Business Administration in Marketing, George Mason University, Fairfax, Virginia . December 1986.

Bachelor of Arts in English, South Hampton College, Long Island, New York. June 1975. ⑨

PROFESSIONAL American Marketing Association
AFFILIATIONS George Mason Alumni Association ⑩

Comments: Nothing on this resume stands out and it lacks eye appeal. Paragraphs are too heavy. Word choice is often clumsy and stilted.

LAURA CURTIN

290 Park Avenue
Williamstown, Virginia 22456

703/450-0090 (h)
703/450-2600 (w)

CAREER OBJECTIVE

A position offering opportunity to demonstrate abilities and advance in the field of product planning and research.

CAPABILITIES AND RELATED ACCOMPLISHMENTS

Marketing. Developed and implemented market research program for client which resulted in sales increasing 50 percent over prior year.

—Observed client operations
—Identified customer tastes
—Drafted and administered
  questionnaire
—Designed sample for study

—Trained interviewers
—Developed software for program
—Drafted analysis plan
—Prepared report and made final
  recommendations

Management. Operated a number of fast food restaurants and supervised staffs of up to 30 persons.

—Hired and trained staff
—Developed recruiting
  program
—Trained shift managers
  and other supervisors
—Resolved problems requiring
  immediate action before
  opening

—Created system to highlight
  employee skills and improve morale
—Established incentive programs to
  increase productivity
—Evaluated employee progress and
  reviewed performance
—Worked with accounting and
  local advertising consultants

Planning and Control. Initiated six and twelve month planning cycles to move new facilities from a negative to a positive profit status. Operated 19 percent ahead of profits estimated by franchise firm.

—Established inventory
  control and minimum lead
  time for purchases
—Implemented daily fiscal
  reports to quickly spot problem
  areas

—Broke sales forecasts down by
  product to identify areas requiring
  marketing support
—Informed banker of our
  progress and obtained refinancing
  of loan at more favorable rate

EDUCATION

Master of Business Administration (Marketing), George Mason University, Fairfax Virginia, 1986
Bachelor of Arts (English), South Hampton College, Montauk, New York, 1975

31

FRANK A. OLSON

1497 Green Meadow   Home (703) 938-0081
Vienna, Virginia 22180   Work (703) 889-5427

CAREER OBJECTIVE

Administrate or manage general training and specific areas such as
Crisis Stress Management.

PROFESSIONAL EXPERIENCE

Town of Vienna Police Department   1967 - present
Vienna, Virginia 22180
    Master Police Officer III.
    Fingerprint Computer Technician. Operate a $1.4 million state-of-the-
art automated computer fingerprint system. Performed the benchmark testing
and evaluation of the fingerprint computer system. Assisted in the
planning and organization of a multi-jurisdictional fingerprint
identification section comprised of ten police departments and a filing
system of 125,000 fingerprint cards. Compile office production statistics.
Senior officer responsible for the operation and supervision of personnel,
for the past ten years, in the absence of the supervisor. Identify crime
scene fingerprints and testify as a criminal court expert in the science of
dactolography (fingerprints). Advisor and participant with the United
States Bureau of Standards in the creation of a standard for the National
Interchange of Fingerprint Identification Information and the standard for
the benchmark testing of Automated Fingerprint Systems. Conduct training
of investigators and partrol officers in the operation of an automated
fingerprint system. Coordinate and assist outside agencies in the
operation of the fingerprint computer system.

    Senior Police Officer II.
    Identification Officer. Senior officer in charge of the operation of
the identification section in the absence of the supervisor. Preserve,
process and collect evidence in serious crime scenes. Perform laborotory
tests on crime scene evidence. Prepare and present court displays of crime
scences. Provide special graphics presentations for the office of the
chief of police. Prepare work schedules for an eight man force. Worked in
a darkroom developing and printing black and white photographs. Trained
line supervisors, investigators, and patrol officers, in areas of crime
scene preservation, fingerprinting, photography, criminal law and courtroom
testimony.
    Primary identification officer on the scene of the first mass murder in
the history of Northern Virginia; the first tornado and the first highrise
building colaspe that killed 14 and injured 45 construction workers.
    Produced video, 16mm movie and slide presentations on police related
subjects. Talked to civic groups and individuals on the topics of home
security and personal protection.

    Juvenile Investigator. Handled cases of criminal child abuse, juvenile
deliquency and crimes committed to and by juveniles. Provide guidance and
assistance to troubled youngsters and their families.

Patrol Officer. Enforced traffic and criminal laws. Interceded in domestic disputes for the purpose of resolving potentially violent confrontations. Provided guidance and information to the public. Trained new officers in proper police techniques of report writing, accident investigation, criminal law enforcement and street survival. Prepared written evaluations to trainees.

United States Army   1965 - 1967
Military Police Specialist E-5. Performed building and operations surveys of military installations. Basic identification procedures, fingerprinting, photography, evidence collection. Investigated requests for financial support for military dependants. Protected dignitaries on visits to military facilities.

Federal Bureau of Investigation   1963 - 1965
Washington, D. C. 22070
Fingerprint Technician. Classified, searched and identified criminals, civilians and foreign nationals. Special assignment fingerprint seracher.
Tour guide. Provided an overview to thousands of visitors to the FBI Laborotories of their accomplishments towards crime solving.

EDUCATION

Georgetown University
Washington, D. C.
Bachelor of Science in The Administration of Justice   1974
Associates Degree in the Administration of Justice   1972

FORMAL TRAINING

Certified law enforcement instructor for the state of Virginia.

Criminal Investigation

Advanced Administrative Latent Fingerprint

Field Officer Trainer

Basic and Advanced Law Enforcement

SKILLS

Instructor for a year and a half with the Northern Virgnia Community College, Manassas Campus, Manassas, Virginia.
Topic: Law Enforcement Photography

Professional photographer.

ORGANIZATIONS

Northern Virginia Chapter, United Ostomy Association.
    Past Vice President
    Treasurer
    Directors Board
    Fund Raising Chairman

Northern Virginia Chapter, Tandy Computer Users Group.

FRANK A. OLSON

1497 Green Meadow
Vienna, Virginia 22180

Home (703) 938-0081
Work (703) 889-5427

--- (2)

1. Too vague. Needs to be strengthened.

2. The dotted lines are hard on the eye.

3. Inconsistent shift in tense.

4. This is too sensational. As the individual is making a career change, this should be de-emphasized.

5. Does this type of information support the career objective?

6. Paragraphs are too heavy.

CAREER OBJECTIVE

(1) Administrate or manage general training and specific areas such as
Crisis Stress Management.

PROFESSIONAL EXPERIENCE

Town of Vienna Police Department 1967 - present
Vienna, Virginia 22180
    Master Police Officer III.
    Fingerprint Computer Technician. Operate a $1.4 million state-of-the-
art automated computer fingerprint system. Performed the benchmark testing
and evaluation of the fingerprint computer system. Assisted in the (3)
planning and organization of a multi-jurisdictional fingerprint
identification section comprised of ten police departments and a filing
system of 125,000 fingerprint cards. Compile office production statistics.
Senior officer responsible for the operation and supervision of personnel,
for the past ten years, in the absence of the supervisor. Identify crime
scene fingerprints and testify as a criminal court expert in the science of
dactolography (fingerprints). Advisor and participant with the United
States Bureau of Standards in the creation of a standard for the National
Interchange of Fingerprint Identification Information and the standard for
the benchmark testing of Automated Fingerprint Systems. Conduct training
of investigators and partrol officers in the operation of an automated
fingerprint system. Coordinate and assist outside agencies in the
operation of the fingerprint computer system.

    Senior Police Officer II.
    Identification Officer. Senior officer in charge of the operation of
the identification section in the absence of the supervisor. Preserve,
process and collect evidence in serious crime scenes. Perform laborotory
tests on crime scene evidence. Prepare and present court displays of crime
scences. Provide special graphics presentations for the office of the
chief of police. Prepare work schedules for an eight man force. Worked in
a darkroom developing and printing black and white photographs. Trained
line supervisors, investigators, and patrol officers, in areas of crime
scene preservation, fingerprinting, photography, criminal law and courtroom
testimony.
(4)   Primary identification officer on the scene of the first mass murder in
the history of Northern Virginia; the first tornado and the first highrise
(5) building colaspe that killed 14 and injured 45 construction workers.
    Produced video, 16mm movie and slide presentations on police related
subjects. Talked to civic groups and individuals on the topics of home
security and personal protection.

    Juvenile Investigator. Handled cases of criminal child abuse, juvenile
deliquency and crimes committed to and by juveniles. Provide guidance and
assistance to troubled youngsters and their families.

Patrol Officer. Enforced traffic and criminal laws. Interceded in domestic disputes for the purpose of resolving potentially violent confrontations. Provided guidance and information to the public. Trained new officers in proper police techniques of report writing, accident investigation, criminal law enforcement and street survival. Prepared written evaluations to trainees.

United States Army   1965 - 1967
Military Police Specialist E-5. Performed building and operations surveys of military installations. Basic identification procedures, fingerprinting, photography, evidence collection. Investigated requests for financial support for military dependants. Protected dignitaries on visits to military facilities.

Federal Bureau of Investigation   1963 - 1965
Washington, D. C. 22070
Fingerprint Technician. Classified, searched and identified criminals, civilians and foreign nationals. Special assignment fingerprint seracher.
Tour guide. Provided an overview to thousands of visitors to the FBI Laborotories of their accomplishments towards crime solving.

EDUCATION

Georgetown University
Washington, D. C.
Bachelor of Science in The Administration of Justice   1974
⑧ Associates Degree in the Administration of Justice   1972

FORMAL TRAINING

Certified law enforcement instructor for the state of Virginia.

Criminal Investigation

⑨ Advanced Administrative Latent Fingerprint

Field Officer Trainer

Basic and Advanced Law Enforcement

SKILLS

Instructor for a year and a half with the Northern Virgnia Community College, Manassas Campus, Manassas, Virginia.
Topic: Law Enforcement Photography

Professional photographer.

ORGANIZATIONS

Northern Virginia Chapter, United Ostomy Association.
Past Vice President
Treasurer
Directors Board
Fund Raising Chairman

Northern Virginia Chapter, Tandy Computer Users Group.

Comments: While this individual has had increased responsibility, a chronological resume does not work for a change to a training position. The resume as it exists highlights police work. There have been many training experiences and these need to be emphasized. A recruiter will not hunt for them.

Frank A. Olson

1497 Green Meadow, Vienna, Virginia 22180   (h) 703/938-0081   (w) 703/889-5427

Career Objective

A position as a training specialist in private industry working with staff development.

---

10 years of training experience in all aspects of police operation:

- Conduct training programs for investigators and patrol officers in the operation of an automated fingerprint system.
- Train line supervisors, investigators, and patrol officers in crime scene preservation, fingerprinting, photography, criminal law, and courtroom testimony.
- Produce video, 16mm movie, and slide presentations on crime scene preservation and fingerprinting.
- Prepare and present speeches on home security and personal protection to civic groups and individuals.
- Train new officers in proper police techniques in report writing, accident investigation, criminal law enforcement, and street survival.
- Taught Law Enforcement Photography at local community college.

20 years of increased responsibility with the Town of Vienna Police Department:

- Manage a 1.4 million state-of-the-art automated computer fingerprint system.
- Specialist in crime scene fingerprint identification and testify as criminal court expert in the science of dactolography (fingerprints).
- Manage the operation and supervision of 65 police officers in absence of supervisor.
- Assist in the planning and organization for a multi-jurisdictional fingerprint identification section comprised of ten police departments and a filing system of 125,000 fingerprint cards.
- Perform the benchmark testing and evaluation of the fingerprint computer system.
- Advisor and participant with the United States Bureau of Standards in creation of a standard for the National Interchange of Fingerprint Identification Information and the standard for the benchmark testing of Automated Fingerprint Systems.

Education and Certification:

Georgetown University, Washington, D.C.
  Bachelor of Science in The Administration of Justice, 1974.
  Associate in Applied Science in The Administration of Justice, 1972.

Fairfax County Criminal Justice Academy, Fairfax, Virginia.
  Criminal Investigation, Advanced Administrative Latent Fingerprint, Field Officer Training, Basic and Advanced Law Enforcement.

Certified Law Enforcement Instructor for the state of Virginia.

Professional Organizations:

United Ostomy Association, Northern Virginia Chapter.
  Past Vice-President, Treasurer, Board of Directors, Fund Raising Chairman.

Tandy Computer Users Group, Northern Virginia Chapter.

SANDRA B. MAGEE

1224 Rollings Lane Fairfax, Viginia 23011

CAREER INTEREST

A position with growth potential in the retailing field.

EDUCATIONAL BACKGROUND

Tobe-Coburn School for Fashion Careers, Certificate of Completion, 1984.

CAREER RELATED COURSEWORK

Retailing; Fashion History; Fabrics; Fashion Promotion; Business Writing; Effective Displays; Public Relations; Introduction to Computers.

WORK EXPERIENCE

Hecht Company, Washington, D. C.

Head of Stock, 1984 - present

Receive and ticket merchandise and set up displays in the women's sportswear department. Take inventory, transfer merchandise, and keep records of department sales. Coordinate all advertising; mount advertising, set up display and ensure adequate stock of merchandise.

Bloomingdale's, Tysons Corner, Virginia

Salesclerk, 1983-1984

Arranged merchandise, re-stacked shelves, and rang up customer sales. Assisted customers and took inventory. Advised management of special requests and set up displays.

The Clothes Horse, Fairfax, Virginia

Salesclerk, 1982

Assisted customers in their purchases, arranged displays, unpacked merchandise and took inventory. Opened and closed the store when the manager was not available.

Fairfax Toyota, Fairfax, Virginia

Receptionist, 1981

Part-time receptionist. Answered phones and directed calls. Greeted and directed customers.

REFERENCES FURNISHED UPON REQUEST

SANDRA B. MAGEE

1224 Rollings Lane Fairfax, Viginia 23011

(1) CAREER INTEREST

A position with growth potential in the retailing field. **(2)**

EDUCATIONAL BACKGROUND

(3) Tobe-Coburn School for Fashion Careers, Certificate of Completion, 1984.

(4) CAREER RELATED COURSEWORK

Retailing; Fashion History; Fabrics; Fashion Promotion; Business Writing; Effective Displays; Public Relations; Introduction to Computers.

WORK EXPERIENCE **(5)**

Hecht Company, Washington, D. C.

Head of Stock, 1984 - present

Receive and ticket merchandise and set up displays in the women's sportswear department. Take inventory, transfer merchandise, and **(6)** keep records of department sales. Coordinate all advertising; mount advertising, set up display and ensure adequate stock of merchandise.

Bloomingdale's, Tysons Corner, Virginia

Salesclerk, 1983-1984

Arranged merchandise, re-stacked shelves, and rang up customer sales. Assisted customers and took inventory. Advised management of special requests and set up displays.

The Clothes Horse, Fairfax, Virginia

Salesclerk, 1982

Assisted customers in their purchases, arranged displays, unpacked merchandise and took inventory. Opened and closed the store when the manager was not available. **(7)**

Fairfax Toyota, Fairfax, Virginia

Receptionist, 1981

(8) Part-time receptionist. Answered phones and directed calls. Greeted **(9)** and directed customers.

(10) REFERENCES FURNISHED UPON REQUEST

1. Career Interest doesn't sound as committed as Career Objective.

2. This is too vague. What type of position in retailing?

3. Where is the school located? A fashion school in New York City has more prestige than one in Minneapolis.

4. This area can be effective and provide support of various skills and knowledge. It should be longer and can be separate or tied into education.

5. The word "experience" by itself is more concise.

6. This can be beefed up. What are the volumes? Both number of pieces and sales revenue. Is this a main store with branches?

7. This area has more responsibility than expressed — expand.

8. Omit the word "part-time".

9. If this area can't be expanded, eliminate.

10. Is this necessary? Use the space to present qualifications.

Comments: Presents candidate as weak on experience and skills. Expand education to support career objective. Develop work experience.

SANDRA B. MAGEE

893-0044

1224 Rollings Road   Fairfax, Virginia 23011

------CAREER OBJECTIVE--

A position as Assistant Buyer or Department Manager in a fashion
retail operation.

-----------------------------EDUCATION--

Tobe-Coburn School for Fashion Careers, New York, New York.
Certificate of Completion, Retailing and Fashion Promotion, 1984.

EDUCATIONAL HIGHLIGHTS

- Assistant Supervisor, Infants at Macy's, Herald Square, New York.
  Spring 1984 work block.

- Salesclerk, Better Dresses at Bloomingdale's, New York, New York.
  Christmas 1983 work block.

- 27 credits in:

Retailing	Business Writing	Introduction to Business
Fashion History	Public Relations	Introduction to Computers
Fabrics	Effective Displays	Fashion Promotion

-----------------------------EXPERIENCE---

Hecht Company, Washington, D.C.   1984 - present
Head of Stock

Coordinate all merchandise for Women's Sportswear department. Receive,
ticket, and transfer merchandise; record, update, and report on department sales. Display merchandise, coordinate advertising and ensure
successful promotions by maintaining proper stock levels.

Bloomingdale's, Tysons Corners, Virginia   1983 - 1984
Salesclerk

Assisted customers, arranged merchandise, re-stocked shelves and handled
cash and credit sales transactions in the Sportswear department. Communicated special requests and trends to management, took inventory, and
set up displays.

The Clothes Horse, Fairfax, Virginia   1982
Salesclerk

Full range of responsibilities in small retail operation. Opened and
closed store in manager's absence, unpacked and ticketed merchandise,
arranged displays and assisted customers in selection and cash and
credit sales transactions.

YOLANDA WILLIAMS
26 Congress Street
Jackson, Mississippi 55006
(226) 889-1142

EMPLOYMENT

Peterson and Lane, Inc.
Jackson, Mississippi

Vice-President	Elected May 1985
Senior Account Executive	November 1984 to Present
Assistant Vice-President	Elected May 1983
Account Executive	January 1982 to November 1984

Senior Account Executive responsible for coverage design, marketing and negotiating with underwriters, interfacing with clients to maintain, administer and coordinate international risk management programs and integrate with domestic coverage placements.

Current clients represent full spectrum of American Multinational Fortune 500 and 1000 Companies: professional services, design construction, engineering, chemical and food industries.

Personally responsible for international premium volume of 6.4 million dollars

International Life Underwriters, Jackson, Mississippi

Casualty Manger	January 1979 to January 1982
Senior Underwriter	June 1977 to January 1979

Responsible for managing, budgeting, personnel, planning, and coordinating casualty underwriting department. Created branch office underwriter training program. Participated in International Life Underwriters Executive "Fast Track" program.

International Life Underwriters
New York, New York

Junior Underwriter	January 1977 to June 1977
Casualty Underwriter Trainee	June 1975 to January 1977

Assisted underwriters in the review, evaluation selection, acceptance, pricing and servicing of casualty accounts. Became familiar with foreign insurance regulations. Developed knowledge and experience in rating procedures/manual usage and underwriting skills. Participated in the International Life Underwriters Career Training Program.

40

EDUCATION

>   NEW YORK UNIVERSITY - B. S. Languages, 1975
>
>   >   School of Languages and Linguistics
>   >   Dean's List
>   >   Cumulative Average: 3.42
>   >   Area of Concentration: Spanish
>
>   UNIVERSITY OF MADRID, Spain - Junior Year Abroad Program, 1973-74
>
>   Cultural Exchange visit to Mexico - Summer, 1972

CAREER RELATED EDUCATION

>   Insurance Principles and Practices, sponsored by International
>   Life Underwriters Education Department, accredited by the College
>   of Insurance, New York.
>
>   Counselor Selling, Wilson Learning Corporation.
>
>   Effective Business Writers, College of Insurance, New York.
>
>   Fundamentals of Finance and Accounting for the Non-Financial
>   Executive, The Wharton School of the University of Pennsylvania.

YOLANDA WILLIAMS
26 Congress Street
Jackson, Mississippi 55006
(226) 889-1142

EMPLOYMENT

1. Inconsistent. Either have the city and state all on one line or under the organization.

2. Omit highlighted months.

3. Use active voice.

4. Omit months.

5. Use active voice.

6. Expand managed and personnel.

7. Inconsistent. Why is one training program in quotes and the other isn't?

8. Use active voice.

(1) Peterson and Lane, Inc.
Jackson, Mississippi

Vice-President	Elected May 1985 (2)
Senior Account Executive	November 1984 to Present
Assistant Vice-President	Elected May 1983
Account Executive	January 1982 to November 1984

(3) Senior Account Executive responsible for coverage design, marketing and negotiating with underwriters, interfacing with clients to maintain, administer and coordinate international risk management programs and integrate with domestic coverage placements.

Current clients represent full spectrum of American Multi-national Fortune 500 and 1000 Companies: professional services, design construction, engineering, chemical and food industries.

Personally responsible for international premium volume of 6.4 million dollars

(1) International Life Underwriters, Jackson, Mississippi

Casualty Manger	January 1979 to January 1982 (4)
Senior Underwriter	June 1977 to January 1979

(5) Responsible for managing, budgeting, personnel, planning, (6) and coordinating casualty underwriting department. Created branch office underwriter training program. Participated in International Life Underwriters Executive "Fast Track" (7) program.

International Life Underwriters
New York, New York

Junior Underwriter	January 1977 to June 1977
Casualty Underwriter Trainee	June 1975 to January 1977

(8) Assisted underwriters in the review, evaluation selection, acceptance, pricing and servicing of casualty accounts. Became familiar with foreign insurance regulations. Developed knowledge and experience in rating procedures/manual usage and underwriting skills. Participated in the International Life Underwriters Career Training Program. (7)

EDUCATION (10)

(11) NEW YORK UNIVERSITY - B. S. Languages, 1975

    School of Languages and Linguistics
    Dean's List
    Cumulative Average: 3.42
    Area of Concentration: Spanish

(12) UNIVERSITY OF MADRID, Spain - Junior Year Abroad Program, 1973-74

    Cultural Exchange visit to Mexico - Summer, 1972

CAREER RELATED EDUCATION

    Insurance Principles and Practices, sponsored by International
    Life Underwriters Education Department, accredited by the College
    of Insurance, New York.

    Counselor Selling, Wilson Learning Corporation. (13)

    Effective Business Writers, College of Insurance, New York.

    Fundamentals of Finance and Accounting for the Non-Financial
    Executive, The Wharton School of the University of Pennsylvania.

(14)

9. Omit.

10. Spell out degree. Don't abbreviate.

11. Include city and state.

12. Format these the same as the above education.

13. There needs to be consistency. Include the city and state where training occurred.

14. Too much white space.

Comments: Needs a career objective or summary to tie this together. Lacks consistency in format. Verbs in the passive voice are weak and don't support the skills and experience needed for upward mobility.

YOLANDA WILLIAMS

26 Congress Street, Jackson, Mississippi 55006   (226) 889-1142

CAREER HIGHLIGHTS

- 11 years of casualty and risk management experience
- Expertise in designing coverage to meet an industry's unique needs
- Manage client base of Fortune 500 and 1000 companies
- Experience with foreign insurance regulations

EXPERIENCE

Peterson and Lane, Inc., Jackson, Mississippi.

Vice-President	Elected 1985
Senior Account Executive	1984–present
Assistant Vice-President	Elected 1983
Account Executive	1982–1984

Design coverage, market, and negotiate with underwriters. Maintain, administer, and coordinate international risk management programs and integrate with domestic coverage placements.

Current clients represent full spectrum of American multinational Fortune 500 and 1000 companies: professional services, design construction, engineering, chemical, and food industries.

Personally responsible for international premium volume of 6.4 million dollars.

International Life Underwriters, Jackson, Mississippi.

Casualty Manager	1979–1982
Senior Underwriter	1977–1979

Opened and managed branch casualty underwriting department. Hired exempt personnel, developed standards of performance, supervised, appraised performance, counseled, and dismissed staff. Planned annual budget of 3 million dollars.

Brought in 20 new accounts. Developed department from one to four person staff. Created branch underwriter training program. Participated in International Life Underwriters Executive Fast Track program.

International Life Underwriters, New York, New York.

Junior Underwriter	1977
Casualty Underwriter Trainee	1975–1977

Reviewed, evaluated, selected, accepted, priced, and serviced casualty accounts while assisting underwriters. Gained understanding of foreign insurance regulations. Developed knowledge and experience in rating procedures/manual usage and underwriting skills. Participated in the International Life Underwriters Career Training program.

EDUCATION

New York University, New York, New York.
Bachelor of Science in Languages, 1975.
 Area of Concentration: Spanish
 Dean's List

University of Madrid, Madrid, Spain.
Junior Year Abroad Program, 1973–1974.

Cultural Exchange Visit, Mexico.
Summer, 1972.

PROFESSIONAL TRAINING

Insurance Principles and Practices, International Life Underwriters, accredited by the College of
 Insurance, New York, New York.

Counselor Selling, Wilson Learning Corporation, New York, New York.

Effective Business Writers, College of Insurance, New York, New York.

Fundamentals of Finance and Accounting for the Non-Financial Executive, the Wharton
 School of the University of Pennsylvania, Philadelphia, Pennsylvania.

LICENSES

Mississippi Brokers License

ASSOCIATIONS

American Association of Casualty Underwriters
Casualty Underwriters Training Council

—— Maria H. Diaz ——
98 Locust Avenue, Los Angeles, California   (213) 778-4556

Professional Experience

1979 - present	Part-time Instructor in Mathematics, Los Angeles Junior College, Los Angeles, CA. Subjects taught: Elementary Algebra, Intermediate Algebra, Trigonometry, Finite Math, Math for General Education. I have also researched and chosen textbooks for Finite Math and Math for General Education.
1976 - 1979	Adjunct Instructor in Mathematics, Los Almos Community College, Los Almos, CA. Subjects taught: Elementary Algebra, Trigonometry, Pre-Calculus. I also worked with students taking self-paced course options.
1974 - 1976	Home Tutor, Thompkins Board of Education, Thompkins, CA. Taught all subjects to students in grades 7-12 who were unable to attend school. I worked with teachers, parents, as well as students, in coordinating their school work.
1974 - 1976	Substitute Teacher, Thompkins Board of Education, Thompkins, CA.
1969 - 1970	Mathematics Teacher, Los Angeles Board of Education, Los Angeles, CA. Taught students in grades 7 and 8 of all abilities.
1968 - 1969	Mathematics Teacher, Orange County Board of Ed-Education, San Francisco, CA. Taught students in grades 9 and 10 of all abilities.

Educational Background

1967 - 1968	Master of Education in Mathematics, including 15 credits in advanced mathematics. University of California, Berkeley, California.
1963 - 1967	B. A. Major: Education Minor: Mathematics (33 credits) State University College, Geneseo, New York

Additional Educational Experiences

1984 - 1985   Auditting Calculus 65A and 65B, Los Angeles Junior
               College, Los Angeles, California.

1984   BASIC Programming Course, Continuing Education,
               Los Angeles, California.

1979   Fortran Computer Science Course, Los Almos State
               College, Los Almos, California.

1976 - 1978   Nineteen credits in Accounting Classes, Los Almos
               Community College, Los Almos, California.

Certification

California Community College Credential in Mathematics
New York Teaching Credential for Mathematics, Grades 7 to 12

Professional Associations

California Mathematics Council for Community Colleges
Mathematics Association of America

Community Activities

Volunteer Mathematics Enrichment Teacher, C. L. Terry Elementary
   School, 1980-1985.
C. L. Terry PTA President, 1983-1985.
C. L. Terry PTA Historian, 1982-1983.
Morris Junior High PTA Historian, 1982-1983.
Girl Scout Leader, 1977-1985.
Age Level Consultant for the Los Angeles Girl Scout Service
   Unit Team, 1982-1985.
Treasurer, Los Almos State College Figure Skating Club, 1977-1979.
Chairperson of Religious School Committee, Los Almos, CA, 1976-1979.

Placement Credentials are on file at: Career Planning and Placement
                                          State University College
                                          Geneseo, NY 12405

— Maria H. Diaz —————————————————————
98 Locust Avenue, Los Angeles, California   (213) 778-4556

Professional Experience

1979 - present   ① Part-time Instructor in Mathematics, Los Angeles
Junior College, Los Angeles, CA. Subjects taught:
Elementary Algebra, Intermediate Algebra, Trigon-
ometry, Finite Math, Math for General Education.
I have also researched and chosen textbooks for
Finite Math and Math for General Education.

1976 - 1979   ② Adjunct Instructor in Mathematics, Los Almos
Community College, Los Almos, CA. Subjects
③ taught: Elementary Algebra, Trigonometry, Pre-
Calculus. I also worked with students taking
self-paced course options ④

1974 - 1976   ② Home Tutor, Thompkins Board of Education,
Thompkins, CA. Taught all subjects to students
in grades 7-12 who were unable to attend school.
⑩ I worked with teachers, parents, as well as students, in coordinating their school work.

1974 - 1976   ⑤ Substitute Teacher, Thompkins Board of Education,
Thompkins, CA.

1969 - 1970   Mathematics Teacher, Los Angeles Board of Education,
Los Angeles, CA. Taught students in grades 7 and
⑨ 8 of all abilities.

1968 - 1969   Mathematics Teacher, Orange County Board of Ed-
Education, San Francisco, CA. Taught students in
grades 9 and 10 of all abilities.

Educational Background

1967 - 1968   ⑥ Master of Education in Mathematics, including 15
credits in advanced mathematics. University
⑧ of California, Berkeley, California.

1963 - 1967   ⑦ B. A. Major: Education
Minor: Mathematics (33 credits)
State University College, Geneseo, New York

1. Eliminate the word "part-time" — experience is experience whether it is full-time, part-time, paid, or unpaid.

2. Either the position or the organization should be highlighted.

3. "Taught" is redundant.

4. Eliminate pronouns.

5. This should have some explanation.

6. Degree and school should be separate and on different lines.

7. Spell out Bachelor of Arts.

8. Inconsistent. Format all education the same.

9. Group positions.

10. Margins are wide and out of balance.

48

Additional Educational Experiences

1984 - 1985 ⑪	Auditting Calculus 65A and 65B, Los Angeles Junior College, Los Angeles, California.
1984	BASIC Programming Course, Continuing Education, Los Angeles, California.
1979	Fortran Computer Science Course, Los Almos State College, Los Almos, California.
1976 - 1978	Nineteen credits in Accounting Classes, Los Almos Community College, Los Almos, California.

⑫

11. Spelling error.

12. These experiences are important but they take up more room than the Bachelor's and Master's degrees. Are they more important? Format accordingly.

13. Does this make the individual a more qualified candidate? A more appropriate place for this information may be the application.

Certification

California Community College Credential in Mathematics
New York Teaching Credential for Mathematics, Grades 7 to 12

Professional Associations

California Mathematics Council for Community Colleges
Mathematics Association of America

Community Activities

Volunteer Mathematics Enrichment Teacher, C. L. Terry Elementary
  School, 1980-1985.
C. L. Terry PTA President, 1983-1985.
C. L. Terry PTA Historian, 1982-1983.
⑬ Morris Junior High PTA Historian, 1982-1983.
Girl Scout Leader, 1977-1985.
Age Level Consultant for the Los Angeles Girl Scout Service
  Unit Team, 1982-1985.
Treasurer, Los Almos State College Figure Skating Club, 1977-1979.
Chairperson of Religious School Committee, Los Almos, CA, 1976-1979.

Placement Credentials are on file at: Career Planning and Placement
                                       State University College
                                       Geneseo, NY 12405

Comments: This resume can be effective and easy to read on one page.

MARIA H. DIAZ

98 Locust Avenue
Los Angeles, California 90030

(213)778-4556 (h)
(213)921-7322 (w)

CAREER OBJECTIVE

A position as a mathematics instructor in higher education.

SYNOPSIS OF EXPERIENCE

20 years experience in mathematics education. Subjects taught include:

Elementary Algebra	Trigonometry	Intermediate Algebra
Pre-Calculus	Finite Math	Math for General Education

PROFESSIONAL EXPERIENCE

Mathematics Instructor, 1979–present
Los Angeles Junior College, Los Angeles, California

Adjunct Mathematics Instructor, 1976–1979
Los Almos Junior College, LosAlmos, California

Home Tutor, 1974–1976
Substitute Teacher, 1975–1976
Thompkins Board of Education, Thompkins, California

Mathematics Teacher, 1969–1970
Los Angeles Board of Education, Los Angeles, California

Mathematics Teacher, 1968–1969
Orange County Board of Education, San Francisco, California

EDUCATION

Master of Education in Mathematics, 1968
University of California, Berkeley, California
Includes 15 credits in advanced mathematics

Bachelor of Arts in Education, minor in Mathematics, 1967
State University College, Geneseo, New York
Includes 33 credits in mathematics

Continuing Education:
Audited Calculus 65A and 65B at Los Angeles Junior College;
19 credits in Accounting; BASIC and Fortran

CERTIFICATION

California Community College Credential in Mathematics

New York Teaching Credential for Mathematics, Grades 7 to 12

PROFESSIONAL ASSOCIATIONS

California Mathematics Council for Community Colleges

Mathematics Association of America

Placement Credentials on file at: Career Planning and Placement,
State University College, Geneseo, New York 12045

ANTHONY PERILLO

95240 Highland Lane
Rochester, New York 14617
(716) 451-0866 (H)
(716) 455-3422 (O)

EMPLOYMENT

1979 - Present
MONROE COUNTY
Internal Audit Division
15 Bell Highway
Roachester, NY 14602

Auditor III-Current responsibilities include primary
supervision of financial, management, and compliance
audits of general fund and other County agencies.
Responsibilities included in these audits are:
 .assigning staff
 .preparation of preliminary survey
 .preparation of audit program
 .performance of fieldwork
 .workpaper preparation
 .progress briefings with the auditee
 .review of all deficiency findings
 .review and approval of audit report
 .training junior audit staff
 .preparation of sampling plan used in test
 work.
Additional duties include working with the
audit director in preparation of the following:
 .work with the County Executive and his
  deputies on special assignments
 .long range audit plan
 .internal audit manuals
 .budget
 .annual report to the County Executive
 .training of audit staff
 .determination of proper utilization of
  junior audit personnel
 .staff performance appraisals
 .audits of County licensed bingo operations

Accomplishments in the field of
accounting/auditing:
 .wrote accounting manual for use by a
  County agency in dealing with grants (sub
  grantees)
 .assisted in writing a Bingo Accounting
  Guide
 .currently studying to finish passing the
  Certified Internal Auditor Exam

 .have taken courses in basic EDP and COBOL
 .attended seminars in contract fraud,
  operational audits, fraud audits, EDP
  auditing, report writing, internal control
  review, communicating audit findings, use
  of statistical sampling in auditing.

1978 - 1979 PAUL G. TRAP, LTD. PO Box 5477 Rochester, NY	Senior Staff Auditor. Responsibilities included Auditor-in-Charge of CETA, Federal Credit Unions, and HUD audits. Training of other staff personnel for audit of government grants. Monthly client write-up and review. Consultation with clients (primarily non-profit) on effective accounting systems, budetary procedures, and preparation of manuals. In addition, supervision and preparation of management and compliance audits were a major part of the position.
1977 - 1978 SELF-EMPLOYED	Responsible to clients which were non-profit, retail, service, and individual tax returns. Experience includes audits for Department of Labor (CETA), Housing and Urban Development, and Federal Credit Unions in the areas of internal audit, budget preparation, computerized books, and all other accounting/auditing functions.
1975 - 1977 ASSOCIATES FOR BETTER ROADS 1199 St. Paul Blvd. Rochester, NY	Employed as Comptroller and Office Manager Responsibilities included contracts and funds received for federal and private foundation grants, direct and indirect costs, and all other phases of accounting operations.

EDUCTION

1970 - 1974	Rochester Institute of Technology
	Rochester, NY
	   Degree: DCS
	   Major: Accounting

ANTHONY PERILLO

95240 Highland Lane
Rochester, New York 14617
(716) 451-0866 (H)
(716) 455-3422 (O)

1. Use active voice.

2. These are all tasks in the audit function and read like a job description.

3. Omit until you have passed the entire exam — then include under certification.

4. Use a separate section to indicate professional training.

5. Accomplishments are hidden.

6. Too much white space.

7. Omit address. It leaves you open to prospective employers randomly calling previous employers for references.

13. Misspelled word.

1979 - Present
MONROE COUNTY
Internal Audit Division
⑦ 15 Bell Highway
Roachester, NY 14602
⑬

⑥

EMPLOYMENT
①
Auditor III-Current responsibilities include primary supervision of financial, management, and compliance audits of general fund and other County agencies. Responsibilities included in these audits are:
 .assigning staff
 .preparation of preliminary survey
 .preparation of audit program
 .performance of fieldwork
 .workpaper preparation ②
 .progress briefings with the auditee
 .review of all deficiency findings
 .review and approval of audit report
⑤.training junior audit staff
 .preparation of sampling plan used in test
  work.
Additional duties include working with the audit director in preparation of the following:
 .work with the County Executive and his
  deputies on special assignments
 .long range audit plan
 .internal audit manuals
 .budget
 .annual report to the County Executive
 .training of audit staff
 .determination of proper utilization of
  junior audit personnel
 .staff performance appraisals
 .audits of County licensed bingo operations

Accomplishments in the field of accounting/auditing:
 .wrote accounting manual for use by a
  County agency in dealing with grants (sub
  grantees)
 .assisted in writing a Bingo Accounting
  Guide
③.currently studying to finish passing the
  Certified Internal Auditor Exam

④ .have taken courses in basic EDP and COBOL
 .attended seminars in contract fraud,
  operational audits, fraud audits, EDP
  auditing, report writing, internal control
  review, communicating audit findings, use
  of statistical sampling in auditing.

1978 - 1979 PAUL G. TRAP, LTD. PO Box 5477 Rochester, NY	Senior Staff Auditor. Responsibilities **(8)** included Auditor-in-Charge of CETA, Federal Credit Unions, and HUD audits. Training of other staff personnel for audit of government grants. Monthly client write-up and review. Consultation with clients (primarily non-profit) on effective accounting systems, budetary procedures, and preparation of manuals. In addition, supervision and preparation **(9)** of management and compliance audits were a major part of the position.	**8.** "Responsibili- ties" is redundant and in the passive voice. Choose ac- tive verbs.
1977 - 1978 **(12)** SELF-EMPLOYED	Responsible to clients which were non-profit, retail, service, and individual tax returns. Experience includes audits for Department of Labor (CETA), Housing and Urban Development, and Federal Credit Unions in the areas of internal audit, budget preparation, computerized books, and all other accounting/auditing functions.	**9.** Weak — use: supervised and prepared man- agement and compliance audits.
1975 - 1977 ASSOCIATES FOR BETTER ROADS 1199 St. Paul Blvd. Rochester, NY	Employed as Comptroller and Office Manager Responsibilities included contracts and funds received for federal and private foundation grants, direct and indirect costs, and all other phases of accounting operations.	**10.** Typo. Should be "BS". **11.** Indicate only the year degree was received. **12.** Accounting Consultant sounds more professional.

EDUCTION

(11) 1970 - 1974	Rochester Institute of Technology
	Rochester, NY **(10)**
	  Degree: DCS
	  Major: Accounting

Comments: This resume is out of balance. The paragraphs are too narrow and too heavy. It has poor eye appeal and is difficult to read. The resume reads like a job description. There are accomplishments but they are hidden. This resume could easily fit on one page and effectively emphasize accounting credentials.

ANTHONY PERILLO

95240 Highland Lane, Rochester, New York 14617   (h) 716/451-0866 (o) 716/455-3422

OBJECTIVE   An audit management position in private industry.

EXPERIENCE

1979
to
present

Audit Supervisor, Monroe County, Rochester, New York.

Supervise and conduct financial management and compliance audits of county agencies for a large local government with an annual budget in excess of one billion dollars. Conduct special assignments for senior county management. Wrote an accounting manual used by grant recipients. Co-authored an accounting guide for nonprofit organizations conducting bingo games and raffles.

1978–1979   **Senior Staff Auditor,** Paul G. Trap, Ltd., Rochester, New York.

Prepared and supervised federal compliance audits for Comprehensive Employment Training Act (CETA), Federal Credit Unions, and Housing and Urban Development (HUD) grants. Trained staff to comply with grant requirements. Provided management advisory services to clients in accounting systems design, required budget practices, and procedures manuals.

1977–1978   **Accounting Consultant,** Rochester, New York.

Provided accounting services to clients on a consulting basis. Client base consisted of nonprofit organizations, retail, and service industry. Assisted in the areas of internal audit, budget preparation, and conversion to computerized systems. Prepared individual tax returns.

1975–1977   **Comptroller,** Associates for Better Roads, Rochester, New York.

Handled contracts and funds for federal and private foundation grants, direct and indirect costs, and all additional accounting operations.

EDUCATION

Bachelor of Commercial Sciences in Accounting, 1974.
Rochester Institute of Technology, Rochester, New York.

**PROFESSIONAL
   TRAINING**

Seminars by the Institute of Internal Auditors: Contract Fraud, Operational Audits, Fraud Audits, EDP Auditing, Report Writing, Internal Control Review, Statistical Sampling, and Communicating Audit Findings.

ASSOCIATIONS

Association of Governmental Accountants
Institute of Internal Auditors

Louise J. Silver   RESUME
89 Kings Park Ridge
Evans, Oregon 09422   Special Educator
  (717) 894-0700 (h)
  (717) 544-8772 (w)

GENERAL BACKGROUND AND SKILLS

Eight years of experience in the field of special education; diagnosis
and remediation of specific learning disabilities, development and
implementation of specialized curriculum for the mentally retarded,
program modification for students with learning disabilities, kindergarten readiness testing. Strong organizational and communication
skills.

EXPERIENCE

1981 - present   Young Adult Institute, Evans and Buhl, Oregon
                   Program Resource Specialist

Responsibilities include development of curriculum, co-leading specialty
groups, evaluating appropriateness of programming through the Utilization
Review process, program compliance with state regulations. Developed
systems for record keeping. Established student internship program with
local colleges. Developed and carried out Program Evaluation system and
Community Education/Outreach program. Responsible for writing and submission of grant proposals. Direct care with profound MR. multiply-
handicapped adults.

1980 - 1981   Allegheny Central School, Allegheny, Oregon
                   Special Teaching Assignment

Teacher for home-bound profoundly retarded child. Responsibilites
included developing and carrying out daily program instruction and
home management. Skills stressed included sustained eye contact,
grasp, balance, awareness of sounds, touch, and self.

1980 - 1981   BOCES, Buhl, Oregon (Evans Central School)
                   Teacher for Resource Room

Responsibilities included development of program goals. Diagnosed and
remediated specific disabilities; recommended program modifications for
students in main-streamed classes. Prepared students for RCT in reading,
writing, and mathematics.

1976 - 1980   BOCES, Allegheny and Evans Central Schools
                   Temporary and Substitute Teacher

Long-term assignments in primary grades; developed teaching strategies
and modified curriculum for disadvantaged children. Substituted in all
grades in elementary school and special education classes for the trainable and educable mentally retarded.

CERTIFICATION   Special Classes of the Mentally Retarded and N-6
                   Permanent, Oregon

EDUCATION   M. S., Education; Oregon State
                   B. S., Education & Behavioral Science, Mercy College,
                   Evans, Oregon

Louise J. Silver
89 Kings Park Ridge
Evans, Oregon 09422
  (717) 894-0700 (h)
  (717) 544-8772 (w)

RESUME ①

Special Educator

1. Omit. This looks like it was copied from a book and the page heading was included.

2. The purpose of this area is to emphasize skills. When the paragraph is heavy and not easy to read — this defeats the purpose.

3. Too much in passive voice. Lacks authority.

4. Shift in tense.

5. Spell this out.

6. Redundant. Too many redundancies take away from the skills and accomplishments. "Developed" is used seven times!

7. Passive voice and redundant.

8. This work location and the one below are not consistent with the first two.

9. What is this?

10. Where is the school located?

11. These two schools and degrees should be formatted the same.

12. Don't abbreviate the degrees.

13. Passive voice. Use active verbs.

14. Passive voice. Use active verbs.

15. Heavy paragraphs are not easy to read.

GENERAL BACKGROUND AND SKILLS

②⑮ Eight years of experience in the field of special education; diagnosis and remediation of specific learning disabilities, development and implementation of specialized curriculum for the mentally retarded, program modification for students with learning disabilities, kindergarten readiness testing. Strong organizational and communication skills.

EXPERIENCE

1981 - present   Young Adult Institute, Evans and Buhl, Oregon
                Program Resource Specialist ③

⑭ Responsibilities include development of curriculum, co-leading specialty groups, evaluating appropriateness of programming through the Utilization Review process, program compliance with state regulations. Developed ④ systems for record keeping. Established student internship program with ⑥ local colleges. Developed and carried out Program Evaluation system and Community Education/Outreach program. Responsible for writing and submission of grant proposals. Direct care with profound MR. multiply-handicapped adults. ⑤

1980 - 1981   Allegheny Central School, Allegheny, Oregon
                Special Teaching Assignment

Teacher for home-bound profoundly retarded child. Responsibilites ⑦ included developing and carrying out daily program instruction and home management. Skills stressed included sustained eye contact, grasp, balance, awareness of sounds, touch, and self.

1980 - 1981   BOCES, Buhl, Oregon (Evans Central School)
                Teacher for Resource Room

⑬ Responsibilities included development of program goals. Diagnosed and remediated specific disabilities; recommended program modifications for students in main-streamed classes. Prepared students for RCT in reading, writing, and mathematics. ⑨

1976 - 1980   BOCES, Allegheny and Evans Central Schools ⑧
                Temporary and Substitute Teacher

Long-term assignments in primary grades; developed teaching strategies and modified curriculum for disadvantaged children. Substituted in all grades in elementary school and special education classes for the trainable and educable mentally retarded.

CERTIFICATION   Special Classes of the Mentally Retarded and N-6
                Permanent, Oregon

EDUCATION   ⑪ M. S., Education; Oregon State ⑩
          ⑫ B. S., Education & Behavioral Science, Mercy College, Evans, Oregon

Comments: This resume is written in the passive voice and lacks authority. This is a highly skilled and trained individual and yet this doesn't come across. Experience and skills need to be developed and presented clearly.

LOUISE J. SILVER
89 Kings Park Ridge
Evans, Oregon 09422

(717) 894-0700 (h)
(717) 544-8722 (w)

—CAREER HISTORY—

- Eight years of experience in special education.
- Diagnosis and remediation of specific learning disabilities.
- Development and implementation of specialized curriculum for mentally-retarded.
- Program modification for students with learning disabilities.

—EXPERIENCE—

Program Resource Specialist
Young Adult Institute, Evans and Buhl, Oregon   1981–present

Ensure compliance with state regulations for day treatment program for 270 mild to profoundly mentally retarded multiply-handicapped adults. Design curriculum, co-lead specialty groups, and evaluate program appropriateness through Utilization Review Process. Write and submit grant proposals.

Established student internship program with local colleges, created and implemented Program Evaluation system and Community Education/Outreach program. Administered direct care. Devised systems for record keeping.

Special Teaching Assignment
Allegheny Central School, Allegheny, Oregon   1980–1981

Teacher for home-bound profoundly mentally retarded child. Established a daily program of instruction and home management. Stressed skills in sustained eye contact, grasp, balance, awareness of sounds, touch, and self.

Resource Room Teacher
BOCES, Evans Central School, Buhl, Oregon   1980–1981

Developed program goals and recommended program modifications for students in main-streamed classes. Diagnosed and remediated specific disabilities. Prepared students for Regional Competency Test (RCT) in reading, writing, and mathematics.

Temporary and Substitute Teacher
BOCES, Allegheny and Evans Central Schools, Buhl, Oregon   1976–1980

Long-term assignments in primary grades. Planned teaching strategies and modified curriculum for disadvantaged children. Substituted in all grades in elementary school and special classes for the trainable and educable mentally retarded.

—CERTIFICATION—
Special Classes of the Mentally Retarded and N–6—Permanent, Oregon

—EDUCATION—
Master of Science in Education
Oregon State University, Buhl, Oregon.   1970.

Bachelor of Science in Education and Behavioral Science
Mercy College, Evans, Oregon.   1967.

Juliette R. Miller (Julie)   Home Phone: (301) 887-0009
7765 Harvest Lane   Office Phone: (202) 655-9982
Chevy Chase, Maryland 25542

PROFESSIONAL EXPERIENCE AND SKILLS

Communications
Negotiate for graphic arts services with commercial and government clients.
Supervise layout and printing of publications and reports.
Write technical proposals for government graphics and printing projects.
Prepared promotional material for educational programs.
Graphic presentation of technical reports.
Patient evaluation reports.
Public relations liaison for Womens Clinic.
Planned, and conducted workshops.

Sales and Marketing
Identified need for marketing of commercial accounts.
Implemented sales program.
Developed promotional marketing strategies.
Generate new accounts.
Promoted services of medical clinic.
Multi-media marketing presentations.
Equine sales.

Graphic Arts -- A/V Production
Designed graphics and layout for brochures and publications.
Artistic consultant to associations for promotional material.
Served as staff artist.
Experienced in use of graphics production equipment.
Illustration and graphics for publication in Medical Journals.
Visual aids for educational conferences and seminars.

Administrative
Project Manager.
Commercial Manager for Medical Group.
Accounting - Accounts Receivable.
Managed Five Acres Farm.

EMPLOYMENT HISTORY

Account Executive 1983-present	Graphics Plus 4566 K Street, NW Washington, D. C. 20001
Account Executive 1981-1983	Image, Inc. 67 West Street, NW Washington, D. C.
Account Representative 1979-1981	Professional Presentations 1009 Bath Street Bethesda, Maryland 20098
Office Manager 1976-1979	Drs. R. Miller and B. Paul 788 Shady Lane Bethesda, Maryland 20098
Counseling Staff 1975-1976	Planned Parenthood Clinic 5688 14th Street, NW Washington, D. C. 20006
Counseling Staff 1974-1975	Northwest Clinic 1809 F Street Washington, D. C. 20007
Self Employed	Five Acres Farm 90 Easy Road Beltsville, Maryland 29001
Medical Graphic Artist 1968-1971	Womans Hospital Akron, Ohio
Assistant Account Executive 1955-1957	B & K Advertising San Francisco, California

EDUCATION

A.A., Graphics and Commercial Design -- Endicott Junior College,
Beverly, Massachusetts
Diploma, Graphic Design, The Parsons School of Design, New York,N.Y.
Art History, New York University, New York, N.Y.
(Degree requirements substantially completed)

COMMUNITY INTEREST ORGANIZATIONS

International Horse Show Committee
Potomac Hunt Club Committee

1. If you want to be known by a nickname, use it.

2. It is obvious this is a phone number.

3. What direction or position is this individual seeking?

4. All of this reads like a list.

5. Too vague. This is in the past and sounds like the present.

6. Incorrect punctuation.

7. How?

8. None of these show how they were done — or what the accomplishments were.

9. Don't abbreviate.

10. There is no meat here.

11. Format is not appealing.

12. These skills are all vague. Need more specifics. What are the results/accomplishments?

13. Too much white space.

Juliette R. Miller (Julie) ①
7765 Harvest Lane
Chevy Chase, Maryland 25542

Home Phone: (301) 887-0009 ②
Office Phone: (202) 655-9982

③   PROFESSIONAL EXPERIENCE AND SKILLS

<u>Communications</u>
  Negotiate for graphic arts services with commercial and government clients.
④ Supervise layout and printing of publications and reports.
  Write technical proposals for government graphics and printing projects.
  Prepared promotional material for educational programs.
  Graphic presentation of technical reports.
⑤ Patient evaluation reports.
  Public relations liaison for Womens Clinic.
⑥ Planned, and conducted workshops.

<u>Sales and Marketing</u>
  Identified need for marketing of commercial accounts. ⑦
  Implemented sales program.
  Developed promotional marketing strategies.
⑧ Generate new accounts. ⑦
  Promoted services of medical clinic.
  Multi-media marketing presentations.
  Equine sales.
                    ⑨
<u>Graphic Arts -- A/V Production</u>
  Designed graphics and layout for brochures and publications.
  Artistic consultant to associations for promotional material.
⑪ Served as staff artist.
  Experienced in use of graphics production equipment.
  Illustration and graphics for publication in Medical Journals.
  Visual aids for educational conferences and seminars.

<u>Administrative</u>
  Project Manager.
⑫ Commercial Manager for Medical Group. ⑩
  Accounting - Accounts Receivable.
  Managed Five Acres Farm.

⑬

EMPLOYMENT HISTORY

Account Executive
1983-present

⑭ Graphics Plus
4566 K Street, NW
Washington, D. C. 20001

Account Executive
1981-1983

Image, Inc.
67 West Street, NW
Washington, D. C.

Account Representative
1979-1981

Professional Presentations
1009 Bath Street
Bethesda, Maryland 20098

Office Manager
1976-1979

Drs. R. Miller and
       B. Paul
788 Shady Lane
Bethesda, Maryland 20098

Counseling Staff
1975-1976

Planned Parenthood Clinic
5688 14th Street, NW
Washington, D. C. 20006

Counseling Staff
1974-1975

Northwest Clinic
1809 F Street
Washington, D. C. 20007

Self Employed

Five Acres Farm
90 Easy Road
Beltsville, Maryland 29001

Medical Graphic Artist
1968-1971

Womans Hospital
Akron, Ohio

Assistant Account Executive
1955-1957

B & K Advertising
San Francisco, California

EDUCATION

⑮ A.A., Graphics and Commercial Design -- Endicott Junior College,
Beverly, Massachusetts
Diploma, Graphic Design, The Parsons School of Design, New York, N.Y.
Art History, New York University, New York, N.Y.
(Degree requirements substantially completed) ⑯

COMMUNITY INTEREST ORGANIZATIONS

⑰ International Horse Show Committee
Potomac Hunt Club Committee

14. Don't use addresses.

15. Spell out degree.

16. This should be worded better — Quantify.

17. These are hobbies — don't tie in with professional interests.

Comments: Resume sounds like a list—this is what I did! Where is the individual going? This is a good example of outlining all of your background without focusing on a direction. Determine the direction and then develop areas to show why they are capable of filling that position.

JULIE R. MILLER

7765 Harvest Lane, Chevy Chase, Maryland 25542

(301) 887-0009 (H)
(202) 655-9982 (W)

OBJECTIVE

A management position in creative services which includes the purchase of support services, artistic consultation, research, and coordination of projects monitored to completion.

PROFESSIONAL EXPERIENCE

Creativity

- Conceptualize and design slide/tape presentations for key clients. Perform detail analysis of clients needs. Analyze data from script and develop graphic design and layout.
- Coordinate artistic direction in choice of graphics, color, and slide format.
- Educate client to purpose and effective use of visual aids.
- Design graphics for print media including promotional material for conventions, charts/graphs for medical journals, posters, magazine advertising, and brochures.
- Created effective visual presentations to customer satisfaction which resulted in repeat business, customer referrals, and top sales award.

Management

- Manage project through design, production, proofing, and final approval.
- Identify and resolve problems, intepretation, production, photographic process, and computer availability to meet client needs.
- Coordinated IBM project involving 500 slides, a 12-minute multi-image audio-visual presentation, and training video tape.
- Developed slide presentations on Tax Analysis and Strategy for Coopers & Lybrand.
- Program and design slides for several divisions at Marriott Corporation.

Marketing

- Analyze business requirements and prepare product and service demonstrations appropriate to client needs.
- Researched market base and developed a marketing strategy to service potential customers. New clients included IBM, Mobil Oil Corporation, Marriott Corporation, and American Satellite Company.
- Doubled client base within 3 years.

EMPLOYMENT HISTORY

Account Executive
1983–present   Graphics Plus, Washington, D.C.
1981–1983   Image, Inc., Washington, D.C.

Account Representative
1979–1981   Professional Presentations, Bethesda, Maryland

Office Manager
1976–1979   Doctors Miller and Paul, Bethesda, Maryland

Counseling Staff
1975–1976   Planned Parenthood Clinic, Washington, D.C.
1974–1975   Northwest Clinic, Washington, D.C.

Self Employed
1971–1975   Five Acres Farm, Beltsville, Maryland

Medical Graphic Artist
1968–1971   Womans Hospital, Akron, Ohio

Assistant Account Executive
1955–1957   B & K Advertising, San Francisco, California

EDUCATION

Endicott Junior College, Beverly, Massachusetts.
Associates in Applied Arts, Graphics and Commercial Design.

Parsons School of Design, New York, New York.
Diploma in Graphic Design.

New York University, New York, New York.
Course work towards a Bachelors Degree in Art History.

PROFESSIONAL ORGANIZATIONS

National Association of Female Executives

Women in Communication

VALERIE WEIL

25 Court Street
Madison, Wisconsin 768005
Home Phone: (502)886-0944
Work Phone: (502)883-1614

CAREER OBJECTIVE
A position as an Administrative Assistant that is challenging and will
lead to greater opportunity and more responsibility.

EDUCATION
1986 Katharine Gibbs School, Madison, Wisconsin
      Administrative Assistant Program

1984 Katharine Gibbs School, Madison, Wisconsin
      Entree Program

1978-1983 University of Wisconsin, Madison, Wisconsin
      Bachelor of Arts in elementary education

WORK EXPERIENCE
Secretary: Association of Airline Transportation (AAT) - 1986
            I worked in the capacity of secretary in the Air Traffic
            Management Department where I worked for a director and
            two managers with duties that included:organizing con-
            ferences and meetings, being responsible for record man-
            agement, prioritizing assignments, implementing ideas
            and strategies daily, familiarity with Wang word processor,
            use of facsimile machine, and the ability to send wires.

Secretary: Reporting Corporation of Airlines (RCA) - 1984 - 1986
            Here I worked in the Financial Recovery Department where
            I worked under a single manager. My responsibilities in-
            cluded: composing correspondences, providing input regard-
            ing policies for office management created and was respon-
            sible for record management, coordinated and compiled diverse
            information (semi-annual report), trained staff and explained
            concepts, took dictation, handled financial aspects such as,
            checks and letters of credits, composed and sent memo of agency
            termination, paid-in-full or bankruptcy claims, and handled
            telephone correspondences.

Assistant Teacher: Madison's Child Development Center - 1983 - 1984
            Here I was an assistant teacher to the 3, 4, and 5
            year olds. My responsibilities included: supervising
            the children in their play, projects, and learning
            skills.

1. Eliminate the word "phone".

2. It's fine to look for opportunity and responsibility — by re-phrasing "more responsibility and greater opportunity." it sounds less self serving.

3. Combine these two.

4. Present experience should be in present tense — not past.

5. Awkward sentence structure and run on sentences.

6. Correspondence is already plural and does not have an "s".

7. Passive voice. Use active voice.

8. Awkward sentence — Eliminate first four words.

9. Too heavy.

10. Paragraphs are too heavy.

11. Don't use pronouns.

VALERIE WEIL

25 Court Street
Madison, Wisconsin 768005
(1) Home Phone: (502)886-0944
Work Phone: (502)883-1614

CAREER OBJECTIVE
(2) A position as an Administrative Assistant that is challenging and will lead to greater opportunity and more responsibility.

EDUCATION
1986 Katharine Gibbs School, Madison, Wisconsin
(3)   Administrative Assistant Program

1984 Katharine Gibbs School, Madison, Wisconsin
      Entree Program

1978-1983 University of Wisconsin, Madison, Wisconsin
           Bachelor of Arts in elementary education

WORK EXPERIENCE
Secretary: Association of Airline Transportation (AAT) - 1986
            I worked in the capacity of secretary in the Air Traffic
(4)   Management Department where I worked for a director and
            two managers with duties that included:organizing con-
(10)   ferences and meetings, being responsible for record man-
            agement, prioritizing assignments, implementing ideas
            and strategies daily, familiarity with Wang word processor,
            use of facsimile machine, and the ability to send wires.

Secretary: Reporting Corporation of Airlines (RCA) - 1984 - 1986
            Here I worked in the Financial Recovery Department where   (5)
(11)   I worked under a single manager. My responsibilities in-
            cluded: composing correspondences, providing input regard-
            ing policies for office management created and was respon-
(9)   sible for record management, coordinated and compiled diverse
            information (semi-annual report), trained staff and explained
            concepts, took dictation, handled financial aspects such as,
            checks and letters of credits, composed and sent memo of agency
            termination, paid-in-full or bankruptcy claims, and handled
            telephone correspondences. (6)

Assistant Teacher: Madison's Child Development Center - 1983 - 1984
            (8) Here I was an assistant teacher to the 3, 4, and 5
            year olds. My responsibilities included: supervising
            the children in their play, projects, and learning
            skills.
                                                    (7)

Comments: Skills need to be highlighted. Writing is awkward and overshadows the experience. Uneven white space. Not easy to read. Experience needs to support career objective.

VALERIE WEIL

25 Court Street, Madison, Wisconsin 768005   (502) 886-0944 (Home)
(502) 883-1614 (Work)

Career Objective

An administrative position that is challenging and will lead to greater responsibility and opportunity.

Skills

- Typewriting, 70 words per minute.
- Shorthand, 50 words per minute.
- Word processing training on IBM Displaywriter and Wang VS-85 System.
- Ability to operate dictaphone and facsimile machine.

Education

Katharine Gibbs School, Madison, Wisconsin
Administrative Assistant Program, 1986.
Entree Program, 1984.

University of Wisconsin, Madison, Wisconsin
Bachelor of Arts in Elementary Education, 1983.

Experience

Secretary, Association of Airline Transportation (AAT), Madison, Wisconsin.
1986–present
Support director and 2 managers in the Air Traffic Management Department. Organize conferences and meetings, create and maintain file systems, prioritize assignments and implement ideas and strategies. Familiar with Wang word processor, use of facsimile machine, and the ability to send wires.

Secretary, Reporting Corporation of Airlines (RCA), Madison, Wisconsin.
1984–1986
Secretary to manager of Financial Recovery Department. Composed correspondence, provided input regarding policies for office management, created and was responsible for record management. Coordinated and compiled diverse information (semi-annual reports), trained staff and explained concepts. Coordinated financial aspects such as checks and letters of credit from travel agencies, communicated and updated agency terminations, accounts and bankruptcy claims and handled telephone correspondence.

Assistant Teacher, Madison's Child Development Center, Madison, Wisconsin.
1983–1984
Supervised 25 pre-school children in their learning skills, projects and recreation.

Associate Memberships

World Airlines Clubs Association
National Trust for Historic Preservation

LYYNE PLANES

12 Hollywood Avenue, Eastchester, New York 10707   (914) 968-8357

Career Objective

A responsible and challenging position in the field of career development and training.

Experience

Westchester County Office of Adult Education, White Plains, New York

Career Planning Program Specialist, 1983 - present

Coordinate and schedule career planning program for county adult education. Develop courses, manage program, recruit, interview and hire instructors. Designed career counseling program, developed alternative career workstyles, entrepreneurship, career exploration and job hunting preparation.

Instructor, 1982 - present

Develop curriculum and teach Job Hunting Techniques, Resumes, Interviewing Techniques, Job Leads, Networking, Part-Time Career Opportunities, Cross-roads for Women, and the Professional Image.

GTE Telenet, Stamford, Conneticut

Technical Writer, 1983

Wrote administrative procedural manual for new billing system. Gathered information through interviews, group meetings, and liaison with other consultants. Designed binders, ordered supplies, coordinated typing, proofing, copying and distribution of manual.

Xerox Corporation, Rosslyn, Virginia

District Billing Manager, 1979 - 1980

Managed billing department for five branch offices. Direct responsibility for staff of ten; recruited, supervised, developed position descriptions, created and utilized training material, established performance criteria and appraised performance.

Office Services Supervisor, 1978 - 1979

Supervised administrative secretarial communication network for 22 secretaries supporting 200 managers. Established support position guides, performance standards, and secretarial handbooks. Conducted awareness seminars, team building workshops, and third party counseling.

Marriott Corporation, Bethesda, Maryland

Credit Manager, 1978

Managed credit department for Contract Food Services Division. Approved credit, resolved billing and credit problems and collected outstanding receivables. Staff of one.

Xerox of Canada, Toronto, Ontario

Customer Services Manager, 1975 - 1977

Developed and implemented credit and collection programs and maintained cash flows. Staff of seven.

Major Account Administrator, 1974 - 1975

Coordinated and implemented a new major account price plan; developed procedures, initiated changes in corporate policy, developed and gave administrative presentations to customers, sales, and administration.

Major Account Coordinator, 1973 - 1974

Initiated collection programs for major accounts. Resolved billing and collection problems.

Xerox Corporation, Syracuse, New York

Credit and Collection Correspondent, 1972 - 1973

Developed expertise in credit and collection procedures.

Education

George Mason University, Fairfax, Virginia

Bachelor of Arts, English. 1980.

York University, Toronto, Ontario

Attended 1973-1975.

Monroe Community College, Rochester, New York

Associate in Applied Arts, Liberal Arts. 1969.

Management Development at Xerox; Management Studies, New Manager Seminar, Managing for Motivation, Management Action Workshop.

Professional Affiliations

American Society of Training and Development
Association of Part-Time Professionals

1. Strengthen career objective.

2. What does the first experience have in common with the third? Is there a pattern of a progressive career path or increased responsibility?

3. What are the accomplishments?

4. These indicate a career change. The format makes it look like the individual skipped around a lot.

LYYNE PLANES

12 Hollywood Avenue, Eastchester, New York 10707   (914) 968-8357

Career Objective

(1) A responsible and challenging position in the field of career development and training.

Experience

(2) Westchester County Office of Adult Education, White Plains, New York

Career Planning Program Specialist, 1983 - present

(3) Coordinate and schedule career planning program for county adult education. Develop courses, manage program, recruit, interview and hire instructors. Designed career counseling program, developed alternative career workstyles, entrepreneurship, career exploration and job hunting preparation.

Instructor, 1982 - present

Develop curriculum and teach Job Hunting Techniques, Resumes, Interviewing Techniques, Job Leads, Networking, Part-Time Career Opportunities, Crossroads for Women, and the Professional Image.

GTE Telenet, Stamford, Conneticut

Technical Writer, 1983

(4) Wrote administrative procedural manual for new billing system. Gathered information through interviews, group meetings, and liaison with other consultants. Designed binders, ordered supplies, coordinated typing, proofing, copying and distribution of manual.

Xerox Corporation, Rosslyn, Virginia

District Billing Manager, 1979 - 1980

(4) Managed billing department for five branch offices. Direct responsibility for staff of ten; recruited, supervised, developed position descriptions, created and utilized training material, established performance criteria and appraised performance.

Office Services Supervisor, 1978 - 1979

Supervised administrative secretarial communication network for 22 secretaries supporting 200 managers. Established support position guides, performance standards, and secretarial handbooks. Conducted awareness seminars, team building workshops, and third party counseling.

Marriott Corporation, Bethesda, Maryland

Credit Manager, 1978

Managed credit department for Contract Food Services Division. Approved credit, resolved billing and credit problems and collected outstanding receivables. Staff of one.

Xerox of Canada, Toronto, Ontario

Customer Services Manager, 1975 - 1977

(5) Developed and implemented credit and collection programs and maintained cash flows. Staff of seven.

Major Account Administrator, 1974 - 1975

Coordinated and implemented a new major account price plan; developed procedures, initiated changes in corporate policy, developed and gave administrative presentations to customers, sales, and administration.

Major Account Coordinator, 1973 - 1974

Initiated collection programs for major accounts. Resolved billing and collection problems.

Xerox Corporation, Syracuse, New York

Credit and Collection Correspondent, 1972 - 1973

Developed expertise in credit and collection procedures.

Education

George Mason University, Fairfax, Virginia

(6) Bachelor of Arts, English. 1980.

(8)

York University, Toronto, Ontario

Attended 1973-1975.

Monroe Community College, Rochester, New York

Associate in Applied Arts, Liberal Arts. 1969.

Management Development at Xerox; Management Studies, New Manager Seminar, Managing for Motivation, Management Action Workshop.

(7) Professional Affiliations

American Society of Training and Development
Association of Part-Time Professionals

5. Lack of emphasis causes one position to blend into the other.

6. Eliminate. Include the degrees only. This information takes away rather than adds.

7. These are highlighted the same even though these are different areas. There is a problem with distinction.

8. Too much white space.

Comments: The work experiences are fairly well written and yet this resume does not work. The problem lies in the presentation. What we notice is an obvious shift in career direction rather than the experience. Chronological resumes work best with progressive career advancement. A functional resume would more advantageously emphasize the skills and accomplishments and support the career objective.

LYNNE PLANES

12 Hollywood Avenue
Eastchester, New York 10707
(914) 968-8357

CAREER OBJECTIVE

A challenging training position in private industry, concentrating on management development and career planning

AREAS OF EFFECTIVENESS

Program Development/Administration

- Coordinate and schedule career planning for county adult education program. Develop courses, manage program, recruit, interview, and hire instructors. Experienced 102% growth in student enrollment. Increased course offerings by 50%.

- Designed a career counseling program, developed alternative career workstyles, entrepreneurship, career explorations, and job hunting preparation. Created programs with local high technology and health care industries, offering career exploration at the work site.

- Wrote administrative procedural manual for new billing system. Gathered information through interviews, group meetings, and liaison with other consultants. Designed binders, ordered supplies, coordinated typing, proofreading, copying, and distribution of manual.

- Coordinated and implemented a new major account price plan; developed procedures, initiated changes in corporate policy, developed and gave administrative presentations to customers, sales, and administration.

Training/Teaching

- Develop curriculum and teach training programs in Management Development, Job Hunting Techniques, Resume Writing, Interviewing Techniques, Job Leads, Part-Time Career Opportunities, Crossroads for Women, Networking, and the Professional Image.

- Research material; create handouts, reference tools, and bibliographies.

Management

- Direct responsibility for staffs of 7 to 22; recruited, supervised, developed position descriptions; created and utilized training material; established performance criteria and appraised performance.

- Managed billing department for machine population of 16,000 units and annual revenue of $66 million.

- Developed and implemented credit and collection programs and maintained cash flows for $33 million in annual revenue.

- Supervised administrative secretarial communication network for 22 secretaries supporting 200 managers. Established support position guides, performance standards, and secretarial handbooks. Conducted awareness seminars, team building workshops, and third party counseling.

EMPLOYMENT

✦ *Westchester County Schools*, White Plains, New York

    Career Planning Program Specialist, Office of Adult and Community Education, 1983–present
    Instructor, 1982–Present

✦ *GTE Telenet*, Stamford, Connecticut

    Technical Writer, 1983

✦ *Xerox Corporation*, Rosslyn, Virginia

    District Billing Manager, 1979–1980
    Office Services Supervisor, 1978–1979

✦ *Marriott Corporation*, Bethesda, Maryland

    Credit Manager, 1978

✦ *Xerox of Canada*, Toronto, Ontario, Canada

    Customer Service Manager, 1975-1977
    Major Account Administrator, 1974-1975
    Major Account Coordinator, 1973-1974

✦ *Xerox Corporation*, Syracuse, New York

    Credit and Collection Correspondent, 1972-1973

EDUCATION

✦ *George Mason University*, Fairfax Virginia

    Bachelor of Arts, English, 1980

✦ *Monroe Community College*, Rochester, New York

    Associate in Applied Arts/Liberal Arts, 1969

✦ *Xerox Corporation Management Training*

    Management Studies, New Manager Seminar, Managing for Motivation, Management Action Workshop

PROFESSIONAL AFFILIATIONS

American Society for Training and Development
Association of Part-time Professionals

Bill Henry Thomas
54 Moon Lane
New City, Virginia 23456
H-703-340-9807

WORK EXPERIENCE

January 1985
to
Present

Salesman/Delivery, The Transmission Service
New City, Virginia

Duties include selling products to customers,
picking up orders from distribution center,and
delivering products to customer.

March 1982
to
September 1984

Administrative Manager, Peterson-Jay and Associates
New City, Virginia

Responsible for operation of personnel office.
U. S. and international travel for the purpose
of purchasing products for African countries as
well as the U. S. Met with key decision-makers
to meet this goal.

January 1981
to
October 1981

Salesman, John Hancock Life Insurance
New City, Virginia

Sold and wrote life insurance policies for customers,
met with customers on routine basis in order to review
existing policies, and maintained all insurance records.

June 1963
to
July 1980

Personnel and Industrial Relations Superintendent.
Mobil Oil Operating Company.
Cape Town, South Africa

Responsible for the field of labor relations, personnel
matters for the entire company consisting of 4,000 employees, management/government relations; 1963-1964 -
Workshop Brake rebuilder; 1964 - 1969 - Industrial Relations Officer; 1969 - two months on-the-job training
U. S. Steel Corporation, PA and participated with
their management team in negotiations with the Labor
Unions. 1969 - 1973- Industrial Relations Section
Head; 1973 - 1974 - Assistant to Management; 1974-
1978 - Industrial Relations Superintendent; 1978-
1980 - Consultant to Management on Industrial Relations
matters.

Headed negotiations team regarding labor union agreement
between Mobil Oil Operating Company and Labor Union of
South Africa from 1973-1978.

Annual attendance to the International Labor Organization in Geneva, Switzerland from 1970-1980, participated
in month-long meeting representing the Employers of
South Africa.

September 1956 to April 1961	Driver, <u>Armstrong Rubber Company</u> Chicago, Illinois
	Delivered tires to customers. Was responsible for clerical duties including filing, typing, and answering phone.

EDUCATION

B. A. Liberal Arts, University of Cape Town, Cape Town, South Africa, 1950-1954

University of Chicago, Chicago, Illinois, 1956-1959, English, Philosophy, Labor Relations.

Kennedy University, Kent, Ohio, January 1969-June 1969. Received Certificate in Management and Labor Relations. Courses studied include Management, Labor, English and Business. One month on-the-job training with U. S. Steel Corporation, Pittsburgh, PA.

PERSONAL

Birth Date: January 19, 1933
Marital Status: Married, three children
Health: Excellent

Bill Henry Thomas
54 Moon Lane
New City, Virginia 23456
(1) H-703-340-9807

1. It is not necessary. If only one phone number is included, it would be assumed to be the home number.

2. Passive voice. Use action verbs.

3. What were the results?

4. Unclear. Did you participate in month long meeting once or one month each year from 1970–1980?

5. 1. Too much important information in one large paragraph. 2. Inconsistent with the rest of experience. The other experience begins at most recent and works backward. This one begins with the oldest and works forward. This is in reverse.

6. This is confusing. Is this what the organization does?

7. The dates take up too wide a margin. Months are not necessary.

WORK EXPERIENCE

January 1985 to Present	Salesman/Delivery, <u>The Transmission Service</u> New City, Virginia **(2)**

Duties include selling products to customers, picking up orders from distribution center, and delivering products to customer.

(7) March 1982 to September 1984 — Administrative Manager, <u>Peterson-Jay and Associates</u> New City, Virginia

(6) Responsible for operation of personnel office. U. S. and international travel for the purpose of purchasing products for African countries as well as the U. S. Met with key decision-makers to meet this goal.

January 1981 to October 1981 — Salesman, <u>John Hancock Life Insurance</u> New City, Virginia

Sold and wrote life insurance policies for customers, met with customers on routine basis in order to review existing policies, and maintained all insurance records.

June 1963 to July 1980 — Personnel and Industrial Relations Superintendent. <u>Mobil Oil Operating Company.</u> Cape Town, South Africa

(5) Responsible for the field of labor relations, personnel matters for the entire company consisting of 4,000 employees, management/government relations; 1963-1964 - Workshop Brake rebuilder; 1964 - 1969 - Industrial Relations Officer; 1969 - two months on-the-job training U. S. Steel Corporation, PA and participated with their management team in negotiations with the Labor Unions. 1969 - 1973- Industrial Relations Section Head; 1973 - 1974 - Assistant to Management; 1974-1978 - Industrial Relations Superintendent; 1978-1980 - Consultant to Management on Industrial Relations matters.

(3) Headed negotiations team regarding labor union agreement between Mobil Oil Operating Company and Labor Union of South Africa from 1973-1978.

Annual attendance to the International Labor Organization in Geneva, Switzerland from 1970-1980, participated **(4)** in month-long meeting representing the Employers of South Africa.

(8) Bill Henry Thomas -- 2

September 1956   Driver, Armstrong Rubber Company
to   Chicago, Illinois
April 1961   (9)
                    Delivered tires to customers. Was responsible
                    for clerical duties including filing, typing,
                    and answering phone.

EDUCATION

(10) B. A. Liberal Arts, University of Cape Town, Cape Town, South Africa,
1950-1954

University of Chicago, Chicago, Illinois, 1956-1959, English, Philosophy,
Labor Relations.

Kennedy University, Kent, Ohio, January 1969-June 1969. Received
Certificate in Management and Labor Relations. Courses studied include
Management, Labor, English and Business. One month on-the-job training
with U. S. Steel Corporation, Pittsburgh, PA.

PERSONAL

(11) Birth Date: January 19, 1933
Marital Status: Married, three children
Health: Excellent

8. Repeat of the name and page number are not necessary. Staple a two page resume.

9. This information is so far in the past it can be eliminated as it does not tie in or add to the career direction.

10. Spell out Bachelor of Arts. Do not include the years attended — only the year of graduation.

11. Omit personal information. Eliminate nationality and include citizenship.

Comments: No career objective or career summary. The resume gives no clue to the position that this individual is seeking. Content is weak. What are the skills and accomplishments? Too much white space.

BILL HENRY THOMAS

54 Moon Lane
New City, Virginia 23456
(703) 340-9807

EXECUTIVE EXPERIENCE IN PERSONNEL AND LABOR RELATIONS

Personnel

Managed and directed personnel office for company of 4,000 employees. Direct responsibility for staff of 25 including three section heads.

Oversaw recruiting, interviewing, employee benefits, and preparation of wage and salary scales.

Reviewed all grievances. Decided cases and took corrective action through suspension, warnings, and termination.

Kept employees informed of corporate news and policies through newsletter and radio station.

Created employee job descriptions; ensured fair hiring practices.

Labor Relations

Negotiated with labor unions on the terms and conditions that affected employees. Utilized current financial information on corporate stability and cost of living index.

Ensured terms and conditions of union management agreement were in force; kept management abreast of new labor laws.

Corporate representative at International Labor Organization (ILO) in Geneva, Switzerland for 11 years and at Labor Ministry.

Handled 25 labor agreements. Negotiated and settled five strikes—50% less strikes than previous administration.

Marketing

Arranged purchases for 15–20 African countries; researched and contacted manufacturers of specific consumer goods, negotiated lowest rates, and secured line of credit.

Marketed product from the initial sale, secured product from inventory, and delivered.

Sold, wrote, and reviewed life insurance policies.

EDUCATION

Certificate in Management and Labor Relations.
Kennedy University, Kent, Ohio. 1969.
Internship in U.S. Labor Union Negotiations.
U.S. Steel Corporation, Pittsburgh, Pennsylvania. 1969.
Bachelor of Arts in Liberal Arts.
University of Cape Town, Cape Town, South Africa. 1954.

CITIZENSHIP

United States

CHAPTER 3

THE GREAT COVER UP—OR HOW TO WRITE THOSE LETTERS

The Cover Story

The cover letter introduces you to a prospective employer. A good introduction entices the reader to review your resume. A well written letter and carefully prepared resume represent your best chance that you will make it to the next phase of the employment process—the job interview. Then, you need to switch from the written to the verbal to complete your successful job campaign.

A good cover letter takes no more time to type than a weak letter—and both cost the same amount of first class postage. Furthermore, time you spend writing a good letter may pay off many times as standard phrases and means of expressing your interests and qualifications can be used again and again.

Cover letters fall into three categories:

1. Unsolicated letter.
2. Letters resulting from a referral or some contact.
3. Letter responding to a job advertisement.

The ability to communicate is an important quality employers seek in job candidates. View letter writing as an opportunity for you to show an employer your own skills in written communication.

Format

The most appropriate letter formats are the full block and the semi-block (or modified).

Full Block

_____
_____
_____

_____
_____
_____

_____ :

_____
_____

_____
_____

_____ ,

_____

All of the typing is lined up against the left hand margin.

Semi-Block

_____
_____
_____

_____
_____
_____

_____ :

_____
_____

_____
_____

_____ ,
_____

The address of the writer and the date are indented. The complimentary close and the writer's name are idented and lined up with the above.

Parts of a Letter

Writer's address Date	10905 Willowbrook Lane Tulsa, Oklahoma 73110 October 17, 1987

Dr. Catherine VanArsdale
Manager of Employee Relations
Blackbeard Creamery
450 N Lincoln Street
Oklahoma City, OK 74110

> Inside address, Same as on envelope. Includes name, title, organization, street or box address, city, state, and zip code.

Dear Dr. VanArsdale:

> Salutation. Always begin with "Dear" followed by courtesy title and individual's last name.

Your recent ad in the **Tulsa Chronicle** . . .

My studies at the University of Oklahoma . . .

During summer vacations while in college . . .

You will find a resume of my qualifications . . .

I will be in Oklahoma City on . . .

> Body of letter, single space, skip a line between paragraphs.

> Complementary close, use "Sincerely, Sincerely yours, or Yours truly"

Sincerely,

Richard Talbot

Richard Talbot

> Always sign letter. Type your name under signature.

RT/lht

> Stenographic identification. Use if letter was typed for you. Your initials in Caps, typist in lower case.

Enclosure

> Use "Enclosure or Encl." when you are enclosing a copy of your resume.

Twelve Steps to Effective Writing

1. Type each letter individually. Use an electric typewriter or word processor. If you can't do it yourself, ask a friend or hire a word processing service.

2. Address the employing officer by name and, if possible, by title. Research names in the library or call the company. With so many organizational changes these days it never hurts to call the organization to verify who is presently in the position and double check the spelling and title.

3. Catch the employer's attention by opening your letter with a strong statement. An employer receives hundreds of letters a month and you want yours to be one that is read.

4. Keep your letter short. It should be one page with five to six paragraphs. It will hold the employer's interest and save you substantial time and cost in typing expense.

5. Use the center of your letter to arouse the employer's curiosity by stating brief facts about your experience and accomplishments.

6. Include clues that hiring you will lead to higher production, greater efficiency, or better sales by focusing on the self interest of the person to whom you are writing.

7. Try and include a challenging thought that will cause the employer to feel that meeting with you would be worthwhile even if there are no present openings.

8. Be direct in requesting an interview or state that you will call to arrange a meeting. Letters should ask for something, and the most common thing to request is an interview.

9. Sign and date your cover letter.

10. Plan on mailing a group of letters all at the same time. If you will be mailing 50 letters and you think it will take you one month to complete all 50, date the letters all with the future completion date. When all the letters are completed, mail them. It is too confusing to follow them up if they have been mailed randomly. Also, if you are to receive three job offers, you want them to occur at the same time so that you may judge which is best for you.

11. When mailing a group of letters, prepare one for yourself and mail it with the others. You will have a good idea that the employer has received their letter when you receive yours. Add one day or two to allow traveling through the organization's mail room before you follow-up.

12. When mailing a batch of letters, or even one, try to think when your letter will arrive so as to receive maximum attention. Most employers receive their heaviest mail on Mondays. On Fridays, they may be more concerned with winding up the week rather than investigating new employees. Mail your letter so that it will arrive in employer offices on a Tuesday, Wednesday, or Thursday.

Unsolicited Letters

Unsolicited letters need to be appealing and well written. Ensure that you are directing your letter to the appropriate individual. Double check the spelling of the organization and the individual's name. Here are some tips.

1. Begin with a specific statement concerning the marketplace.
2. Highlight your most marketable skills.
3. State your most recent experience.
4. State your most recent accomplishments.
5. Plan a follow-up.
6. Close your letter on a positive note. "I look forward to speaking with you" because I know that I will be speaking with you. An inappropriate close would be "I hope to speak with you" or "I am anxious to speak with you." The former is too passive and the latter too eager.

See the sample of an unsolicited letter from Patrick Kelly.

Letters from Contact or Referral

The letter needs to be addressed to the individual you have contacted or been referred.

Mention the previous contact or referral in the first paragraph. Do not rely on someone to remember a previous conversation or meeting.

Keep these tips in mind.

1. As you remind the reader about a previous contact or referral, take this opportunity to say something positive about the organization or the position.
2. State your experience that highlights skills that qualify you as a prospective candidate.
3. State your recent accomplishments.
4. Close your letter.

See the sample of a letter from a contact from Carl Boswell.

22 Waverly Street
Denver, CO 44521
January 9, 1987

Mr. William K. Smith
Controller
Atlas Construction
930 First Highway
Denver, CO 44235

Dear Mr. Smith:

Efficient and effective administration of sales and customer service support means good customer relations. Satisfied customers generate more business. I can contribute to your organization's effectiveness by establishing good working relations with customers and personnel at all organizational levels.

My experience during the past eight years of my career has developed skills in:

- organization
- communication
- problem solving
- goal setting

Most recently these skills have been put to use in a multinational corporation developing and implementing collection programs to maintain favorable cash flows, ensuring the validity of customer billings, and administering customer care programs.

Last year, under my direction, my branch exceeded all credit and collection targets and achieved a days sales outstanding of 28 days. My enclosed resume highlights these accomplishments.

Mr. Smith, I will be calling you sometime during the next five days to discuss with you how my skills can be put to use at Atlas Construction.

I look forward to speaking with you.

Yours truly,

Patrick Kelly

Patrick Kelly

Enclosure

42 Palm Road
Miami, FL 32079
May 13, 1986

Dr. Janet Merlino
Dean of Business
Dade Junior College
32 Grenada Boulevard
Miami, FL 32079

Dear Dr. Merlino:

David Fields, senior partner with Wilson, Fields and Brooks, has told me you have an opening for an instructor in your accounting program. I have had the opportunity to review your curriculum and feel I have the qualifications for the position.

I hold a Master of Science degree in Accounting and am a Certified Public Accountant. My ten-year career in public accounting has included clients in both the public and private sector. My background includes two years teaching introduction to Accounting and Auditing with Dade County Adult Education and as a guest lecturer at the University of Miami. Details appear on the attached resume.

I will phone for an appointment and look forward to meeting you.

Sincerely yours,

Carl Boswell

Carl Boswell, CPA

Enclosure

Letters For A Job Advertisement

A letter responding to a job advertisement should follow the basic rules of good cover letter writing. When I was recruiting, we often received over 1,000 resumes in response to a classified job advertisement. How will your letter compete in a stack of 1,000? Make sure you open with an imaginative sentence and draw the reader's attention. These suggestions may help.

1. State the job for which you are applying and where you saw it advertised.
2. Ensure that all of your paragraphs don't begin with pronouns, particularly "I."
3. Comment on the qualifications listed in the advertisement.
4. Match your skills to the required qualifications.
5. State your interest in the job.
6. Carefully respond to all elements of the job or provide all requested information.

See the example of a letter from Regina Goslind.

HELP WANTED

CIRCULATION

SUBSCRIPTION ASSISTANT

Resp. for promotional follow up in subscriptions, through telemarketing & mailings. Req. 1 yr. exper. in telemarketing. Exper. in sales promotion & clerical pos. also helpful.

Send cover letter & resume to: Mr. Rice, Personnel Mgr., Oshkosh Publications, 67 Ash St., Oshkosh, WI 87009. No phone calls or drop-ins please.

---

89 Seymour Way
Oshkosh, WI 87009
June 6, 1989

Mr. Bill Rice
Personnel Manager
Oshkosh Publications
67 Ash Street
Oshkosh, WI 87009

Dear Mr. Rice:

Communication skills are the key to success for the Subscription Assistant position you advertised in Wednesday's **Herald Dispatch.**

My expertise in the following areas qualifies me for this position:

- Excellent oral and written communication skills.
- Two years of telemarketing experience with the Associated Press.
- One-year experience promoting a local weekly publication.
- One year of clerical experience in a retail operation.
- An Associates degree in Liberal Arts with an English major.

The Subscription Assistant position is in line with my career goals, as outlined in my enclosed resume. I would like the opportunity to meet with you and discuss how I will be able to make a contribution to your organization.

Sincerely,

Regina Goslind

Regina Goslind

Encl.

A Dozen More Tips

1. **Numbers**
   - Spell out numbers from 1 to 10.
   - Write figures from 11 upward.
   - Be consistent.
   - Exception: When a number follows a dollar sign ($), always write figures.

2. **Parallelism**

   Related points should be written in the same grammatical form. For example:

Incorrect	**Correct**
development of curriculum	developing curriculum
co-lead groups	co-leading groups
evaluate program compliance	evaluating program compliance
write grant proposals	writing grant proposals

3. Use **Right Hand Justification** for even right hand margins. Electronic typewriters, word processors, and personal computers with word processing software offer justification where lines are automatically spaced to provide an even right hand margin.

4. **Courtesy Title**

   If you are unable to determine the gender of an individual, omit the courtesy title.

   For example:

   Leslie A. Jones
   Dear Leslie A. Jones:

5. If you don't know a woman's preference, use Ms.

6. When answering a classified advertisement that does not give an individual's name, use the following courtesy title:

   Dear Employer:

   This is very positive in that it implies that they will be your employer. It resolves the gender problem and eliminates the old fashioned Madam, Sir, or Gentlemen.

7. Use a 9 1/2 x 4 1/8 business size envelope. The envelope should be the same color and weight of the enclosed paper. Include an outside and return address on the front of the envelope.

8. The outside address should always be the same as the reader's inside address. Line up all lines of the address.

9. Once again, avoid jargon, slang, and abbreviations.

10. The state can be abbreviated both on the inside address of your letter and the outside address of your envelope. Use the acceptable post office abbreviations.

11. Never photocopy a cover letter. It gives the impression that you don't care and don't want to take the time to do it properly.

12. Check and re-check for spelling and typing mistakes. Remember that your letter represents you. A good presentation equals a good image.

BIBLIOGRAPHY

Berman, Eleanor. **Re-entering.** New York, New York: Playboy Paperbacks, 1980. Excellent step-by-step information to prepare yourself to return to work. First hand accounts by women who have successfully re-entered are inspiring.

Bly, Robert W. and Blake, Gary. **Dream Jobs.** New York, New York: John Wiley & Sons, Inc., 1983.
An excellent guide for exploring nine careers that are challenging and fast-growing. Advertising, biotechnology, cable TV, computers, consulting, public relations, telecommunications, training and development, and travel. Covers what it takes, getting started, your first big break, terminology, and lots of resources.

Fader, Shirley Sloan. **From Kitchen to Career.** New York, New York: Stein and Day, 1977.
How-to's for using life experience to bypass clerical positions and step right into management. First hand accounts by women who have successfully made the transition.

Figler, Howard. **The Complete Job Search Handbook.** New York, New York: Holt, Rinehart and Winston, 1979.
A comprehensive and easy to read guidebook. Excellent section on skill/interest exploration and offers valuable job hunting techniques and sources.

Jackson, Tom and Mayleas, Davidyne. **The Hidden Job Market for the 80's.** New York, New York: Time Books, 1981.
Written in workbook style, offers a viable job hunting plan with corresponding exercises. Good working tool.

Staff of CATALYST. **Marketing Yourself.** New York, New York: Bantam Books, 1981.
Guide to resumes and interviews. Section on interviews is very effective. Interesting view giving both the interviewer and the interviewee's thoughts concerning the interview. Helpful tips.

Staff of CATALYST. **What to do With the Rest of Your Life.** New York, New York: Simon and Schuster, 1981.
Valuable guide to career options. Lengthy essays on specific fields and career choices.

Welch, Mary Scott. **Networking.** New York, New York: Warner Books, 1981.
A unique and in-depth source of what networking is, what it offers to career success and job hunting, and how to develop your own.

Wright, John V. **The American Almanac of Jobs and Salaries.** New York, New York: Avon, 1984.
Excellent source for in-depth career exploration and salary ranges.

U.S. Department of Labor. **Occupational Outlook Handbook.** Washington, D.C.: Government Printing Office, 1986.
Excellent guide to 1986–1987 careers; pros, cons, and salary ranges. Organized by professions.

Resume Aids

If the information on resume makeovers has been helpful to you and if you or a friend would like to have your resume reviewed, mail it and the coupon below. For $25.00 you will receive a one page summary of comments, such as those made on the samples in this book. Please allow three weeks for this process.

Resume Aid Order Form

To: Robbie Miller Kaplan
   PO Box 1623
   Vienna, VA 22180

Dear Robbie:

I would like to have my resume reviewed and to receive your suggestions for improvements. My check for $25.00 and my draft resume are enclosed.

   Your name:

   Complete mailing address:

   Telephone number (and area code):

If you would like to order additional copies of this book, use the form below.

To: Garrett Park Press
   PO Box 190B
   Garrett Park, MD 20896

Please send ____ copies of **Resumes: The Write Stuff.** A check or money order for $8.95 per copy is enclosed. (Orders from institutions will be accepted to be billed, but follow normal ordering procedures for your organization.)

   Your name:

   Complete mailing address:
